T0301739

THE CONTROL OF
BUSINESS
RELATIONSHIPS

How
Social Control Theory
Explains
Interactions
Among
Organizations

THE CONTROL OF BUSINESS RELATIONSHIPS

How
Social Control Theory
Explains
Interactions
Among
Organizations

DAVID I GILLILAND
Colorado State University, USA

World Scientific

NEW JERSEY · LONDON · SINGAPORE · BEIJING · SHANGHAI · HONG KONG · TAIPEI · CHENNAI · TOKYO

Published by

World Scientific Publishing Co. Pte. Ltd.

5 Toh Tuck Link, Singapore 596224

USA office: 27 Warren Street, Suite 401-402, Hackensack, NJ 07601

UK office: 57 Shelton Street, Covent Garden, London WC2H 9HE

Library of Congress Cataloging-in-Publication Data
Names: Gilliland, David I., author.
Title: The control of business relationships : how social control theory explains interactions
    among organizations / David I. Gilliland, Colorado State University, USA.
Description: New Jersey : World scientific, [2024] | Includes bibliographical references and index.
Identifiers: LCCN 2023049054 | ISBN 9789811284878 (hardcover) |
    ISBN 9789811284885 (ebook) | ISBN 9789811284892 (ebook other)
Subjects: LCSH: Interorganizational relations. | Social control. |
    Organizational behavior. | Organizational sociology.
Classification: LCC HD57.7 .G553 2024 | DDC 302.3/5--dc23/eng/20231018
LC record available at https://lccn.loc.gov/2023049054

British Library Cataloguing-in-Publication Data
A catalogue record for this book is available from the British Library.

For any available supplementary material, please visit
https://www.worldscientific.com/worldscibooks/10.1142/13639#t=suppl

Desk Editors: Nimal Koliyat/Nicole Ong

Typeset by Stallion Press
Email: enquiries@stallionpress.com

Printed in Singapore

To Colin, Graham, and Mary

About the Author

 **Dave Gilliland**, a professor of marketing at Colorado State University, teaches classes in business customer relationships and marketing research. His research interests focus on governance and control characteristics of inter-organizational exchange, particularly channels of distribution and business-to-business relationships. His research, on these and other topics, has appeared in the *Journal of Marketing* and *The Journal of the Academy of Marketing Science*, among others. Dave just completed an 18-year stretch as a visiting professor at Aston University, Birmingham, UK. He is the editor-in-chief of the *Journal of Inter-Organizational Relationships*. Dave was a CSU Service Learning Scholar and was awarded the Northern Colorado Multicultural Service Award for his work with student service learning projects. Before completing his doctoral work at Georgia State University, Dave worked for over 10 years in industry in marketing, advertising, and marketing research.

Contents

Introduction

Control is ubiquitous. We are all under control, so much so that it isn't recognizable. We are controlled by law; we do not steal, we do not break contracts, and we do not drive over the speed limit (most of the time). We are controlled by religious standards; we do not commit adultery, we are expected to contribute scarce resources to our places of worship, we raise our children to be good citizens. We are controlled by family norms; we eat dinner at 6:00, clothes are handed down from the older siblings to the younger, we visit the grandparents at holidays. We are controlled by the groups in which we are members; we dress in certain ways and cheer for the same team, gang members adorn themselves with like tattoos. Possibly most important of all, we are controlled by our own personal ethics.

We also control others, such as our families, our subordinates, and our students. For all intents and purposes, we are a hub in a complex network of control.

As we begin to think about control, we begin to consider its complexities. First, who is the controller and how is that decided? Who is the target of control? Second, control is dynamic, it changes over time. Consider a family moving through time. There is no doubt that in most young families the parents are the controllers and the children are the targets of control, but as time moves forward and children grow into young adults they gain control of their own lives, making their own decisions. Eventually, as the parents age the children often take over the role of the controller. Thus, control is a fluid concept.

The application of control mechanisms, the processes by which control is attempted, are often in conflict with one another. Management and employees may have very different views of how things should be done, and try to control one another (management tends to control by edict and employees control by establishing shared cultural norms). Other conflicts over control are a bit more serious. Some cultures condone honor killings, the murder of a family member who brings shame to a family. This form of control, known as "self-help," where you take things into your own hands, represents how an acceptable cultural norm can be in conflict with legal rules and the expectations of the general society. Thus, control can be brutal, as in war, while at the same time being socially acceptable.

One question that we will address in a much different setting is whether attempts to control work is intended. Clearly, control works to a certain degree. Laws keep society in check, work rules help assure productivity, regulatory constraints prevent unfair trade, and even honor killings may restore family pride. But control, even when applied by the benevolent, does not imply that it is necessarily good. Thus, why do we follow the rules of control? Why do kids come home by 11 as their father requests? We will examine the consequences of control, which we refer to as sanctions. We receive positive sanctions in the form of incentives to cooperate if we behave — we can borrow the car if we come home on time — or negative sanctions in the form of punishments if we do not. By the way, almost everyone has the right and responsibility to resist control, there just may be consequences if they choose to do so. Thus, control is not about good or bad, right or wrong. It is about the ability to leverage a resource to gain advantage in some way.

The control examples that we have referred to can be grouped into two categories or modes of control. These modes drive the basic understanding of control, what it is and how it is used, and how it might motivate acceptance or rejection from the target. These modes of control can be described as formal or informal. Formal control refers to a usually codified control source held by one in a position of authority (a law, a rule, a contract) designed to achieve a goal. *Informal control* is usually a non-written norm, belief, or expectation, also designed to achieve a goal. The existence of formal and informal controls suggests there may be more than one way to achieve desired outcomes. So, which do we use, and why? It is the comparison and juxtaposition of these multiple modes of control that motivate much of the academic literature on this topic. The notion that control modes, both formal and informal, can be used in tandem, as substitutes, or individually at different times in the same scenario, is one reason the topic is so interesting.

Control is not only ubiquitous, it is necessary to move our personal lives, our jobs, the organizations of which we are members, and, in fact, our countries forward. Societies cannot exist without control mechanisms that advance law, order, compliance, and conformity. Without control there would be chaos and anarchy, as individual self-interests battle for influence. Is control always good; does control always work? Well, no and no. But, since prehistoric times, control has moved families, countries, and civilizations forward, for good or bad.

Control in Business Relationships

These same types of control mechanisms occur in the business world, where one party — firm, consortium, employee group, contractual partner — seeks to use its leverage on another party to gain influence or advantage. In marketing distribution relationships, the original equipment manufacturer (OEM) of a product, say an automobile manufacturer, wants to control the quality of the product and services provided by its dealer network. It knows that as the value of its autos in the eyes of the potential buyer increase, it will earn a higher sales price and margin. Thus, it has a series of inducements to keep the dealer on task and motivated to provide the highest possible level of customer service. These inducements are many, and they range from positive (increased floor plan funding) to negative (reduction in employee discounts for new car purchases), from formal (dealer websites with rules and regulations clearly outlined) to informal (auto dealers that don't comply with attempted control are often surprised to find themselves at the end of the queue when next year's models are distributed).

OEMs also use control mechanisms to try to control their component purchases by doing due diligence during factory tours with prospective suppliers. In supply chains, controls govern the quantity of allowable failures in an incoming shipment. Accounting firms provide audits for clients — in a very formalized way — to ensure the financial situation is as the books claim. Hamburger franchisors own a substantial portion of their own restaurants, instead of franchising them out, to control new product test markets and in-store design elements.

To illustrate the importance and complexities of control, I mention a study done in 2002 (Gilliland and Manning 2002), where Ken Manning and I investigated the relationship between the Larimer County Health Department restaurant inspectors and restaurant managers. Local restaurant owners had organized a letter-writing campaign designed to counter many seemingly poor and unfair restaurant inspections that were doled out by the Health Department. Inspections are tense, high-pressure tests of the extent that a restaurant follows the Health Department food safety codes to keep its customers safe. An inspection goes something like this: The inspector shows up unexpectedly at the back door of the kitchen. They announce they are there for a food inspection and everyone freaks out. The inspector takes about 45 minutes to test the temperatures of the cold holding areas, test the temperatures of the food prior to serving, question employees on proper safety techniques and examine the cleanliness of the kitchen, the sinks, the food preparation counters, and the dining areas. For every violation they find, the inspector deducts points to come up with the total food safety score. A lot is at stake for the restaurant because the results are reported to the newspapers, who write headlines about failed inspections, and are placed on the Health Department's website for diners to review.

Many restaurants complained that they were written up for the smallest and silliest violations, which made them look unfairly poor to the public. Some told me they were losing business because the inspectors inspected strictly by the book with no leeway given. If the cold holding area was one degree over the limit, they would get a violation for supplying unsafe food. Some of the ethnic restaurants complained that there were regulations they couldn't translate, which caused them to lose customers and be threatened with closure.

Clearly, the Health Department had both the diners and the managers' best interests at heart but weren't sure how to keep both groups happy and safe. I was in the middle of a control dilemma.

When riding along with the inspectors the problem became clearer. Often, it wasn't the rules of the inspection that were the problem, it was how the rules were applied. All serious violations tended to be treated similarly among all inspectors, but what mattered were how the smaller violations were handled. Some of the crustier inspectors (one, in fact, was an ex-Marine) played directly by the rules, despite the unimportance of the violation and how it related to the safety of the food served. One restaurant was dinged simply for having an unclear label on a container of food. While this constituted an official violation, it angered the manager that the rules were applied so rigidly. Meanwhile, I witnessed other inspectors talk to employees about how such violations, although they seemed small, could eventually lead to a more serious problem. Just a bit of information was all the employee needed to be aware of the rule in the first place, and remember to mark the next food container appropriately. Thus, my first face-to-face experience with formal and informal control.

While this was an eye-opening experience, the final empirical results were even more compelling. We found that the more the inspectors used informal mechanisms of control (advice, training, explanation), the more the restaurants adhered to the food safety guidelines. Formally applied controls (the letter of the regulation) also motivated compliance, but to a lesser degree. And guess which type of control mechanism resulted in more misrepresentation and overlooking of the inspector's requests? Yes, formally applied control.

Why Study Control?

Business relationships are important to the provision of value in market-based societies. When firms collaborate, they gain economic resources, technological resources, and knowledge-based resources. Collaboration between organizations has been found to be much superior, in most cases, than going it alone (Dekker 2004). Further, as markets expand, firms are not able to cover additional territories on their own and tend to acquire distribution partners. Division of labor suggests that firms specialize and produce unique and sometimes-singular technologies, and that there is a competitive advantage as a result of governance strategies alone (Dyer and Singh 1998). To receive a return for their efforts they must engage in buyer–seller relationships which, when strung together result in various supply chain relationships. Other examples of business relationships include strategic partnerships, agency relationships, and franchise relationships. Any substantive business cannot succeed without bonding relationships with partners. Thus, our question becomes, "How does control work in business relationships?"

Informal conversation has been described in many loose relationships, which are typically transactional in nature. Most relationships, however, are held together by formal stipulations such as those included in written contracts. The contract often specifies how the firms must work together or collaborate. Other business relationships are held together by social norms, friendships, and trust. Trust-based relationships tend to last longer and be more efficient than regular relationships.

Of course, not all business relationships refer to interfirm relationships. Examination of any viable entity will demonstrate the extent of exchange between separate organizations within the firm (intrafirm relationships): manufacturing works with engineering, finance works with upper management, human resources work with operations, and marketing works with just about everyone. Thus, although the majority of this book concerns interorganizational relationships, intraorganizational relationships are also considered (see Chapter 4).

In the majority of interorganizational exchange cases, it is generally accepted that control is necessary for successful — profitable, efficient, and effective — outcomes. But what about those other cases? Control sometimes doesn't work, in fact, control can hurt relationships. Why is this? There are really two questions to consider. First, "Is the appropriate control mechanism being applied?" Perhaps instead of checking *how much* of your product your business partner is selling, you should be monitoring *how* they sell (or *vice versa*). Second, "Is the control mechanism being applied in the correct way?" Will you formally count how successful your partner is in terms of sales, share, or contribution margin, or will you informally work with them to reach a desired outcome?

Inspiration for this Book

I began this book in May, 2022, but have actually been writing it in my head for much longer. As it stands, the control literature is quite disjointed when it comes to business relationships. It is driven by different theories, and each theory uses its own language, methodologies, and assumptions, and comes with its own research stream. I follow the multitheoretic approach in my own writings, using, for example, transaction cost analysis, trust–commitment theory, organizational control theory, governance theory, resource dependence theory, and agency theory. All along I was able to see that we were actually talking about the same things, we were just using different assumptions and languages, or at least dialects.

There were two instances that made things click and started me thinking about an overall, integrating model that would consider most all control incidences across most all theoretic domains. First, when I was working on my dissertation my supervisor, Dan Bello, handed me a conference paper (Lai and Nevin 1995) to read. This paper suggested that control mechanisms — from various theories — could work together to govern particular situations. Of course, they can … in real life they do. I was inspired by this perspective and learned from many authors in the reference list. The second blinding glimpse of the obvious came during my fieldwork for my dissertation. In 1996 I was interviewing Gary Bell, a marketing director for a subsidiary of Kawasaki Heavy Industries, and I asked him about how he used contracts with his dealers. He said the formal contract specified and defined the rules of the relationship. He told me, "When we start the relationship, we go over the contract in great detail, then I put it in a file drawer and don't look at it again until I have to fire them." This instance stayed in the back of my mind, and I still think about it today. In fact, both examples were instrumental in driving my thinking about an organizing control framework that was eventually published in Gilliland (2023). This book is a greatly expanded examination of control, relying on the 2023 framework.

Social Control Theory

One of the most important contributions of this book is to introduce social control theory. Social control theory can actually be described as a meta theory because it is a combination of many governance and control theories. Social control theory is originally derived from the fields of sociology and legal studies, which are interested in combinations of ways to govern most all aspects of society, primarily formal and informal.

Social control theory is used to explain phenomena, establish a control framework, support control models, and make predictions (all the things that a theory should do). By defining "control," social control theory provides a base on which individual governance theories can rest. As the book progresses, social control theory becomes more useful in how we think about issues of control.

Chapter by Chapter

We begin with an overall explanation of social control as control is vital to all business relationships. The roots of social control are in the non-business literature, but a common framework can be applied to a variety of business settings. In Chapter 1, I present the primary interorganizational theories that motivate our understanding of social control. Social control has few assumptions but tackles the complex notion that all economic activity is wrapped in a social context. Chapter 1 concludes with a brief discussion of the similarities of control.

In Chapter 2, I lay out the general framework on which social control theory rests. We will take a quick look at the theory and then introduce the first major component of the theory: the control systems. The three control systems are briefly introduced: self-control, where parties to an exchange control themselves through written mandates and organizational culture, dyadic control, which is explained as control by two parties and, finally, third-party control, control by a party (e.g., a regulatory agency) outside of the focal dyad. We summarize the three systems so differences and similarities might be compared. We also discuss how firms have the right to control others, and begin our book-long examination of whether control works.

In Chapter 3, I examine the history of social control, how it emerged from the study of German society by Tönnies and others.

His work forms the basis for understanding the two modes of social control: formal control and informal control. Each mode is discussed in some detail. I describe the differences in control modes (via the different mechanisms of control) and handle additional topics regarding how control, in the form of its mechanisms, is applied. We close by discussing combinations of modes and mechanisms.

In Chapter 4, we look at the first of the social control systems, self-control. We begin with self-help, which occurs when one attempts to address a conflictual situation with another person or entity. Self-help is the beginning of the control process as organizations manipulate and negotiate terms with their partners. We then examine self-control and its link to control within an organization. Next, we examine theoretical models of motivation, then spend the bulk of the chapter on the mechanisms of the self-control system, with a particular emphasis on corporate culture.

In Chapter 5, we continue our study of the systems of control, particularly as applied to a dyad. The discussion of dyadic control relies heavily on the extant governance and control literature. We thoroughly walk through the mechanisms of control (setting standards, monitoring, sanctioning) with an emphasis on the differences in the formal and informal modes. As part of this section we summarize many influential articles on how incentives often fail, referring to this as the incentive myth. Finally, we delve into the very important notions of trust and shared goals, and how that applies in control relationships, for good and bad.

In Chapter 6, we look at the last of the three social control systems, third-party control. Third-party control mainly concerns control by outside parties, that is, control by parties outside of the transactions and activities of the focal relationship. This means taking deeper dives into regulatory agencies, trade associations, and networks of a certain type. The modes and systems of control still apply, but the context creates new situations for consideration. We also sneak our first peak at two topics that will be a prime focus over the last few chapters: the costs of control and agreement between controller and target.

We shift gears in Chapter 7 to discuss the costs of social control. This chapter starts with an explanation of how different control mechanisms can be used together to complement one another, or possibly be substituted for one another. I summarize the literature, which suggests complementation is the better view. Next, I will suggest that control emerges due to the controller's lowest cost conditions necessary to produce compliance. This chapter provides a full explication of how the rules of control both reduce costs by stopping opportunism and inefficiencies and raise costs due to their implementation and operation. Not all costs are evident and countable, but the idea of costs and control, which I expand, will prove useful.

Our general hypothesis of control drives Chapter 8. We revisit costs and complementation and examine the main determinants of control structure: relationship disposition (goal congruence and dependence), organizational behaviors, industry norms, and risk. These, and other issues, add costs to, or subtract costs from, the control setting, causing changes in the structure of control.

Chapter 9 addresses the main question of the book (does control work?) head-on. It will suggest that control works to the extent that the target of control agrees, based on expected benefits, with the source and plan for control. If there is agreement, control mechanisms are more likely to work. But even when control works, there may be pushback or retaliation by the target. Wrapped in this discussion is our second hypothesis of control. A control profile is then developed that specifies different forms or profiles of control based on agreement and control mode used. Sometimes control works, sometimes it does not.

In the last chapter, I pose questions which might guide control research in the future. The major questions are summarized, and several possible directions are laid out for future examination. Finally, a brief look at how control technologies of the future (e.g., machine learning, artificial intelligence, electronic micro-monitoring) are examined.

Chapter 1

Control

Control is steeped in sociological sciences. Sociology itself, which we might refer to as the birthplace of control, is interested in how people and societies change, adapt, and progress. Those in control of such societies are tasked with providing safety, opportunity, techno-logical advancements, and all the creature comforts of a positive living experience. Of course, this experience is different for every society, as each follows its own path. In many parts of the world, such a path is merely one that attempts to control for safety and the satisfaction of the most basic human needs. In other societies, self-actualization may be attainable to the few and the fortunate.

A quick glance at the news tells us that control has both positive and negative, sometimes very negative, outcomes. Thus, there is no inherent "rightness" to control. An immediate assumption, which we will examine later, is the extent that control is associated with some type of power and authority. What else allows controllers to govern their constituents, or targets, of control? Is there a difference between attempted control and realized control? If so, what is that difference?

The study of control from a sociological standpoint takes us down many paths — control by governments, the police, the military, political parties, our bosses, families, neighbors and neighborhoods, courts and the legal system, regulatory agencies, informal groups of friends, and many more. This book will suggest that control has many similarities across all of these settings, and what we learn from control in one context might be very applicable to the business context which we examine here. One group of similarities will be the possible outcomes that control is designed to produce.

The result sought by control is compliance, which comes in many different forms. When seminar students are assigned a heavy set of readings, they usually choose to comply with the assignment in order to attain the various rewards that accompany such behavior. When county health departments set food safety standards to protect restaurant patrons, the kitchen manager is likely to follow the health department's advice to avoid the associated sets of punishments which accompany non-compliance: low inspection scores, sick customers, and the accompanying poor press. Athletes usually choose to comply with their contractual requirements, patients follow doctor's orders, and we keep our front lawns tidy.

An argument can easily be made that goes like this: of course, we will comply to evade the punishment or earn the incentive that accompanies compliance. But clearly, that isn't always the case, as doctor's orders are often ignored and restaurants cut corners. So, we often ask ourselves, "Should we comply?" What is weighed in that decision? Are there economic rewards/costs that accompany a failure to comply that offset those of compliance? Are there social consequences to be considered?

Usually, as in the cases above, compliance is voluntary, but oftentimes it is forced; the target of control often has no choice but to comply. When the judge rules a certain amount of maintenance is due in the case of divorce, we must comply. But does control necessarily *work*? A perpetrator of a crime sentenced to prison has no choice but to comply. In the case of the prisoner, can we classify the control attempt "successful?" A quick look at the US prison system, which is at more than capacity mainly due to minor drug offenders and vagrancy, might suggest otherwise. Of course, others would argue that prison allows reflection, opportunities to learn, a chance to get away from the influences of the streets, and other elements that make good citizens out of the confined. The outcomes of control, like control itself, are nuanced.

The Control of Business Relationships

Dekker (2004) suggests that it is important to study control in business relationships because of its impact on firm performance. Chen *et al.* (2009) suggest that control is a key element in strategy formulation and implementation. Both formal and informal controls can make a relationship more efficient, more coordinated, and more aligned with positive managerial practice. As we know, inefficiencies and divergent goals pull against an organization and cause confusion in the marketplace and the firm, often leading to failure. In fact, Dekker goes on to describe how interorganizational relationships have high rates of failure, and control can improve this situation.

The context of control

Our setting for the study of control is business relationships, and our targets of control are somewhat different than you'd typically find in a sociological context, as are our goals and measures. We are only interested in sociological control — or anthropological control, psychological control, medical control, or biological control — to the extent it informs our context. Consider Figure 1.1 and many of the interorganizational settings in which control takes place in the business context. The most common are:

- *Buyer–Seller Relationships*: These relationships are a form of agency relationships and are quite basic. A seller of a product or service provides its goods to a firm that uses them in some way. Such relationships are generally held together by a contract of some form that specifies the details of the agreement. Mineral extractors (coal

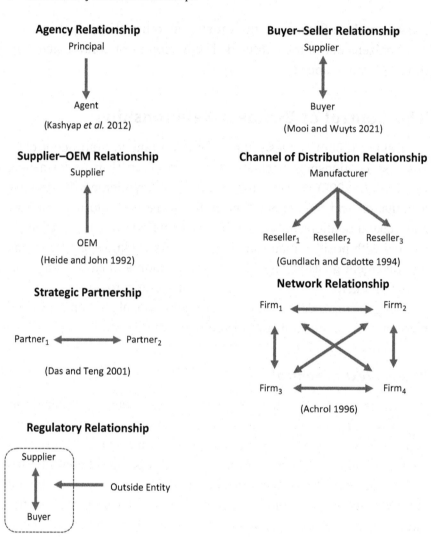

Figure 1.1.   Typical Patterns of Control in Interfirm Relationships

Note: The arrowhead indicates the typical direction of control.

mines, quarries, etc.) sell their product to buyers including aggregate processors. Details of the contract may include the quality of the product sold, delivery requirements, the use of the product, and sometimes legal aspects such as trademark or licensing agreements. Regarding service providers, advertising agencies, attorneys, and accountants sell their services to user firms. These relationships are also contract based. A key aspect of control in business relationships is the authority granted by the written contract.

- *Supplier–OEM Relationships*: These relationships can be considered a subset of buyer–seller exchange or a form of agency relationships. They include a supplier of a component part and an OEM that markets to businesses, governments, or individuals either directly or through an independent distribution network. Consider suppliers of automobile components such as steering columns, transmissions, or window motors and their dealings with large auto manufacturers. Contracts protect both parties from quality failings and missed shipment deadlines. Control can be "up or down" in these relationships as firms seek to protect their interests and leave open the potential for a long-term relationship.
- *Channel of Distribution Relationships*: Every firm has a go-to-market strategy, and thus, a path to the end-user market. The market may consist of retail stores, dealers, distributors, fast food franchises, or other such outlets. Channel relationships are classic control relationships in that they are typically top-down. The supplier (say an OEM, franchisor, or other channel captain) manages a network of dealers to market and sell its products. These relationships are typically held together by complex contracts that provide instruction, guidance, training, incentive, and monitoring information to the dealers. The incentives motivate performance as desired by the supplier, describe how the dealer will be monitored, generally either by financial outcomes or behavioral observation, and how sanctions will be imposed on the dealer, often in the forms of fines and in extreme cases, termination. These types of relationships are typically referred to as "agency relationships."
- *Strategic Partnerships*: Strategic partnerships occur for a variety of reasons including access to additional resources, markets,

distribution, and technologies. Control can be quite interesting in such environments, as firms share risk of failure along with the opportunity for additional revenue. We might refer to control attempts in this setting as "dual control." Each firm wants to control the other and, despite being partners, are sometimes at odds with one another.

- *Network Relationships*: Consider a consortium of firms with a specific task. Perhaps these firms are held together by a common enemy, say foreign importers. Perhaps they have been assembled via a trade association to band together to ward off outside industry threats that are seen as substitutes for their own offerings. We can describe control attempts in this setting as multiple control situations as the members of the network all seek to contribute but are obviously most concerned with their own outcomes. Other settings for network relationships include multidyadic exchange within a certain frame.

- *Regulatory Relationships*: In regulatory relationships, we are not concerned with dyad exchange from the control perspective. In regulatory relationships the controller — usually a regulatory agency or trade association — lies outside of the dyad and attempts to exert control on the dyad (and others). Regulatory relationships are unique in that they involve outside parties to the exchange that often have little financial motivation to gain from their actions. Think of agencies such as the Federal Trade Commission and its attempts to control antitrust violators. Its basis for control is the authority legally granted to it, and the rules and laws that support its existence. Its power source lies in this authority, and it is usually able to achieve its goals not only from the legal courts but also from the courts of public opinion.

- *Supply Chain Relationships*: We can think of supply chain relationships as a series of buyer–seller relationships. Each firm in the chain has the need to control to protect its own interests. It is also controlled by others in the chain. Conflict occurs in supply chains when one firm fails to take charge and other firms negotiate and transfer products down the chain with little coordination.

Of course, not all control contexts are of the interorganizational flavor. We are also interested in intraorganizational control. For instance, groups, departments, suborganizations, and others are involved in the control of others within the same organization. Johnston and Bonoma (1981) showed how, in a buying center for a capital equipment purchase, different departmental organizations attempted to influence other departments to control the purchase decision. Organizations also control themselves via management's posting of firm documents and principles that guide behaviors and activities for employees. Finally, we can even think of corporate culture as an informal controlling influence on how individuals and organizational groups behave.

The theories that drive our understanding of control

A common criticism of the control literature is that it is not always clear (Crosno and Brown 2015). There are several powerful, mature, and well-specified theories that explain control, but each comes with its own sets of assumptions, terminology, control mechanisms studied, and control outcomes. Even research contexts and methodologies used to test relationships are somewhat integral to the individual theory. Although each of these theories offers competing explanations, each is interested in how control is attempted and applied. In most cases, the theories are complementary to one another, although cases occur where theories may predict conflicting outcomes (Krafft 1997). Also, the primary outcome of these theories is how the controller attempts to control its target. Let's briefly examine the primary theories of control.

Transaction Cost Analysis (TCA): In 2009, the Nobel Prize for Economics was awarded to Oliver Williamson for his work on how firms are organized (Williamson 1975, 1996). Williamson, who based much of his work on Ronald Coase's theory of the firm (Coase 1937), wrote that the study of TCA involves whether transactions are carried out in-house in a controlled hierarchy or whether they are executed by a separate organization, the classic make-or-buy problem. Building on foundational work by Coase and Williamson, the study of TCA has sparked work in a variety of interorganizational fields and settings. In general, transaction costs are the costs of designing and running a governance, or control system. These costs include the costs of writing contracts, monitoring performance, and enforcing the relationship (Rindfleisch and Heide 1997). Depending on transaction costs and the costs of production, TCA suggests whether the transaction will be organized within the organization and governed by hierarchical means, or whether it will be organized outside of the firm and governed externally, by a variety of control mechanisms. In summary, the mechanisms of control manage the prime governance problems, the problem of adapting to uncertain environmental conditions, the problem of accurately monitoring performance outcomes (Grewal *et al.* 2010), and the problem of dealing with a partner's opportunistic behaviors. TCA has been applied to international exporting and distribution environments (Klein *et al.* 1990) as well as many other settings in marketing, management, accounting, and supply chains.

Agency Theory. Agency theory is concerned with the writing and maintenance of a work contract between the firm (the principal) and an agent hired to do the firm's bidding (Eisenhardt 1988). The key determinant of the design of the contract is the efficiency of how the exchange is governed. Unlike TCA, agency considers both formal or written contracts and informal or non-written agreements (White 1985). The assumptions of agency, that economic man, (1) is driven by self-interest, (2) works with incomplete information (see Mishra *et al.* 1998), and (3) is affected by uncontrollable environmental factors suggest that there are both pre- and post-contractual problems with alignment. Different risk preferences and conflicting goals emphasize the importance of screening as an efficient solution to the risk of hiring or contracting with another party. The main players in the agency scheme are the principal and the agent. Because goal sets are assumed to be divergent, the principal attempts to align the incentives of the agent to its own, providing motivation and control of the agent's performance. Agent performance is checked and corrected via the principal's monitoring of outcome and behavior (Eisenhardt 1988). A key contribution of agency theory has been the notion of shirking. Similar to opportunism, shirking suggests that workers (employees, dealers, retailers, franchisees) will avoid work if goals are not aligned (Wathne and Heide 2000) and if the cost of avoiding work is less than the costs of being found out (punishment and reputation costs). In agency theory, control is manifested by the principal's offered incentives and its monitoring of the agent's behaviors and outcomes.

Power-Dependence Theory: Few theories have meant more to the interorganizational control literature than power-dependence theory and its many extensions. The study of power, and its mirror, dependence, investigate how an organization's resources contribute to its ability to successfully influence others (Frazier and Summers 1984). Drawing on literature from the sociological research field (French and Raven 1959), Frazier and his colleagues (e.g., Frazier *et al.* 1989) tied a firm's resource-based power to its ability to attempt a variety of influence strategies. Further, the success of the influence attempts was a function of the type of influence strategy used (Payan and McFarland 2005). The literature then became interested in the notion of dependence and mutual dependence (e.g., Scheer *et al.* 2015), finding that dependence, when shared — that is, high levels of interdependence magnitude and asymmetry — led to more collaboration and relational behaviors (Scheer *et al.* 2003). Gundlach and Cadotte (1994) demonstrated how mutual dependence resulted in more non-coercive influence attempts, more relational behaviors, and fewer feelings of residual conflicts.

Contract Law Theory: As you can guess from its title, contract law theory is the theory of contracts, which are generally supported by a legal system. Thus, contracts are usually defensible in a court of law. Contracts are incomplete due to the high costs of writing contracts and the contract-writers inability to predict important contingencies (did anyone think COVID?). A contract is at the heart of an interorganizational relationship as it typically specifies the relationship's activities, duration, and termination. There have been many different conceptualizations of a contract's importance to an interorganizational exchange. One, provided by Gundlach and Murphy (1993) suggests that contracts lie at a nexus between ethical principles and contract law principles. That is, ethics are generally inherent in many contracts. Contracts can be hard (explicit) or soft (normative) and soft contracts are important in driving the existence of relational norms and performance in interorganizational exchange (Lusch and Brown 1996). Also the more specific the contract, the better it is at reducing the transaction costs surrounding the exchange, thus increasing performance (Mooi and Ghosh 2010). Another important issue is the extent and severity that contracts are enforced and how this contributes to the deterrence of illegal activities (Antia *et al.* 2006). Finally, Kashyap *et al.* (2012) find the contract's *ex-ante* completeness is negatively related to *ex-post* incentives and enforcement.

Relational Norms: Macneil (1980) looked at contracts as one end of a continuum of exchange, with the opposite end being relationships. He wrote how contracts drove transactions between organizations as did relationships, but in quite different ways. His focus was on relationships, and he described the basic function of how organizations can work together without the specific guidance of a contract based on reciprocity to one another. Macneil suggests that organizations execute a version of the Golden Rule when a positive deed is returned with a like positive deed. Firms that behave in a reciprocal manner develop norms of exchange over time.

From the early work of Macaulay (1963) we see that contracts may frame how a relationship is structured, but the contract is often kept in the file drawer as the relationship continues under the mutual understanding of the participants. Mutuality, role integrity, and solidarity between parties were found to be drivers of perceptions of fairness (Kaufmann and Stern 1988). Further, relational exchange was shown to be more closely associated with a longer-term orientation than transaction-based exchange (Ganesan 1994, Ring and Van de Ven 1994). Heide and John (1992) further developed the notion of relational norms by considering flexibility between parties and their willingness to exchange proprietary information, certainly a high bar to clear. This chapter importantly notes that bilateral expectations could hold relationships together and increase control over transactions in the relationship. The trust literature produced its own set of marketing and management studies (see the work of Zaheer and colleagues; e.g., Zaheer *et al.* 1998).

Trust–Commitment Theory: Trust–Commitment theory was seminal in advancing our understanding of interorganizational relationships. It suggests that firms that believe in and dedicate themselves to each other will share superior success (Morgan and Hunt 1994). It takes the position that the economy is subsumed in the fabric of the relationship. Commitment, anteceded by trust, binds firms together through credible investments (Anderson and Weitz 1992) and attitudinal bonding (Gilliland and Bello 2002). Interorganizational research exploded in this domain when Morgan and Hunt (1994) introduced the notions of trust and commitment into the literature. This inspired a great deal of work and extensions of their original postulations.

Organizational Control Theory: Organizational control theory is interested in both intra- and interorganizational control. Depending on firm requirements and available information, organizations will control, or attempt to control, in different ways. Ouchi and Maguire (1975) found that managers will, first and foremost, control by observing and modifying employee behaviors (behavioral control) if, and only if, they have adequate knowledge of the means-end process. Without this knowledge — maybe the firm is too large, or the employees' behaviors are hidden in other ways — firms will attempt outcome controls to manage how much of a certain activity is achieved. Outcome controls involve counting, such as units sold, revenue, market share, and customer service scores. Further, outcome and behavioral controls are described as independent and not substitutes or complements of one another. This was confirmed by Anderson and Oliver (1987) but has been debated since. This will be discussed in more detail in later chapters.

When neither output nor behavior controls are available, clan control, control by members of the employees by the employees, is useful (Ouchi 1979). Clan control is based on like-mindedness and fairness (O'Reilly and Chatman 1996). This sounds a lot like relationalism and, in fact, has drawn many comparisons. Jaworski (1988) relied on the Ouchi prescription and brought the notion of formal controls (output and behavioral monitoring) and informal controls into the marketing literature. The idea of formal and informal control was tested and supported (Gilliland and Manning 2002, Jaworski *et al.* 1993) and remains at the heart of the control literature today (see Crosno and Brown 2015, Grewal *et al.* 2013). The main difference in the perspectives of Ouchi and Jaworski is that Ouchi treats controls as substitutes for one another — either output, behavioral, or clan control. Jaworski and others see controls as working together within a singular control framework. We will use the control literature as a primary explanation for our framework of social control.

Incentive Theory: Incentive theory is a spin-off of agency theory; in fact, Gibbons (2005, p. 2) refers to agency theory as the "economic theory of incentives." Incentives are described as monetary and non-monetary inducements that arc designed to compel the agent to perform the principal's tasks effectively and efficiently. Incentives are constructed by the principal to control the agent's behavior. A principal designs the incentive contract to address a constellation of challenges, thus, an incentive package can be thought of as a comprehensive portfolio of individual incentives (Gibbons 2005). See Gundlach and Cadotte (1994) and Gilliland (2003) for an organized list of such incentives. Derivations on the basic theory (see Williamson 1991) have described more about incentives, such as they vary in their ability to convince the intermediary to adopt the incentive package. Known as high-powered and low-powered incentives, some incentives have immediate and typically monetary payoffs, while others are low in power — they have extended payoffs that are not always strictly monetary-based (Obadia *et al.* 2015). Once an incentive package is accepted, and the agent performs as specified, the spectrum of principal needs is met. Thus, similar to agency theory, incentive theory postulates that control is inherent in the incentive portfolio.

Stewardship Theory: Stewardship theory recognizes that sometimes, the goals of the principal and the agent are *not* misaligned, and when this occurs the assumptions of agency theory do not hold, hurting its predictability (Wasserman 2006). In this case, the principal becomes a steward of the relationship and the general outcomes and behaviors of its intermediary. Control is emphasized as being available via both monetary and psychological incentives and as the principal's goals are realized, the agent maximizes its outcomes due to efficient coordination between the two and compliance on the part of the agent. Further, risk is shared between the two parties, decreasing the principal and the agent's exposure to uncontrollable economic circumstances. What conditions might result in mutually shared goals? Gilliland and Kim (2014) found that, among a combined sample of high-technology firms and beer brewers, agreement on strategic direction produced compliance and commitment.

Governance Theory: Governance theory emerged as thoughtful scholars noticed similarities across different theories of how relationships are controlled. In Heide's (1994) seminal piece on governance, he suggested that there are six basic governance mechanisms (the specification of roles, planning, making adjustments, the provision of incentives, monitoring, and enforcing the relationship) used across three primary governance structures, or modes (market governance, unilateral governance, and bilateral governance). This matrix has driven a great deal of work over the last 30 years (e.g., Antia *et al.* 2006, Heide and Wathne 2006) including empiricalization of the basic framework (Gilliland *et al.* 2010). The three modes of governance parallel earlier work by Braddach and Eccles (1989) and their conceptualization of transactions being controlled by the price in the market, authority, or trust. Governance scholars in the management field consider governance mode combinations such as trust and control, or trust and power (Bachmann 2001). The literature tends to coalesce around these modes as general structures to a control relationship, and around incentives, monitoring, and enforcement as some of the specific mechanisms used to control organizations.

Control scholars have many robust and mature theories at hand to explain the phenomena that occur in the field. Each theory has been carefully specified and most have been quantitatively validated with data from practitioners, suggesting external validity. However, each of the different theories comes with its own perspective and assumptions and continues to splinter an already diverse literature. As we look across these many theories, perhaps an effort should be made toward consolidating the similar thoughts on control.

With this as our starting point, this book seeks to provide a common language to the control field by explicating a unifying, organizing framework for control. In doing so I hope to provide higher levels of descriptive, explanatory, and predictive power for our work.

So, What is Control?

Control has long been identified as one of the four key responsibilities of management, along with planning, organizing, and coordinating (Fayol 1949). Merchant (1988, p. 40) puts these four in perspective as he describes the control function as the "back end of the management process where managers attempt to ensure that things are going the way they should." Importantly, this back end includes the establishment, definition, and writing of rules that manage the activities of all parties to an exchange, the motivation for the correct execution of the rules, and ways of forcing adherence to the rules. Although coordination has also been considered as control, it is a bit different as it focuses on planning and organizing functions. Likewise, others have used the term as synonymous with governance, a very broad construct. Still, others describe control as simply an influence on the outcomes and behaviors of the target.

Distinguishing the front end from the back end, and both from daily coordination activities is difficult. Regarding the front end, planning is the organizing of activities in preparation for a transaction. Planning includes selecting and specifying the roles of the actors, planning the processes necessary for success, establishing the rules of authority, and specifying the terms of engagement between the parties. However, before we discount planning completely we should note that planning may be used to establish the existence of behavioral norms, which, in turn set the standards for both relationalism and control. Let's provide a bit more detail on these alternative views of control.

Control, the back end, is where our hands get dirty. It involves establishing the standards, typically via a contract, by which the relationship will be judged, actively monitoring the activities of the target, and providing the necessary rewards and punishments to keep things on track. In the words of Crosno and Brown (2015, control is "monitoring, directing, evaluation, and compensating agents." Das and Teng (2001, p. 258) suggest "in the planning and control framework, control plays the role of checking and making sure that activities are being carried out according to plan." When Merchant refers to "to ensure that things are going the way they should" he may be referencing whether goals are aligned, which is necessary for success. The structure for goal alignment is inherent in the standards and activities of control (Bouillon *et al.* 2006). Finally, based on the goal alignment controls, management accomplishes the day-to-day work of the channel by nudging the target to coordinate appropriate behaviors and outcomes.

An interesting take on social control is how managers direct actions that lead to the effectiveness of the organization. According to Klein's (1989) process model, motivational control begins with goal setting and ends with behavioral change. Agreed, but it is still up to us to describe what is controlled and how.

At this point, it is important to acknowledge a different perspective on control. Some control scholars treat output and behavioral controls as monolithic governance structures where the contract, incentives, monitoring, and enforcement processes are wrapped together as an output control contract or a behavioral control contract (see Bergen *et al.* 1992). As you might expect, an output contract focuses on coordinating goals and activities based on output numbers, and a behavioral contract is based on managing the performance of processes of organization. In fact, Oliver and Anderson (1994) demonstrated how output and behavioral control fell at opposite ends of a continuum between the two. Although the continuum has not been corroborated,[1] it is an interesting way of conceptualizing the large differences in the two methods.

---

[1] In fact, Grewal *et al.* (2013) discuss the often-substantial *positive* correlations between output and behavioral control mechanisms. This relationship has been found in other studies as well.

More specifically, besides Bergen *et al.*'s (1992) notion of outcome and behavioral contracts of combined elements, Jaworski (1988) describes control as "attempts to influence" (p. 26) by formal or informal means. Celly and Frazier (1996) look at outcome and behavioral controls as "attempts to influence" the partner (p. 206). Bello and Gilliland (1997) separate outcome and behavioral control suggesting that outcome control is monitoring, and behavioral control is influence attempted. Eisenhardt (1985) also views control as an influence.

The advantage of our perspective on control is that we break apart the effects of contracts, monitoring and enforcing contracts into separate pieces under one umbrella. We can see how control mechanisms must coordinate with one another. Our view also more clearly demonstrates just how informal control mechanisms fit into our framework. The disadvantage of our perspective is that it doesn't fully explain the manifestation of our control mechanisms, particularly informal control mechanisms.

Another take on a broad-form perspective of control is provided by management scientists Quinn and Rohrbaugh (1983). In their perspective, the term control *per se* is very narrow, but what is broad is their perspective on firm performance, and if we discuss the performance of the organization, we are discussing a need to control. Interestingly, they build their consideration of performance and effectiveness on four models of firm performance.

- *Rational Goal Model*: Effectiveness means the achievement of specific and measurable, usually accounting-based, outcomes such as profit, returns, and sales. Organizations that meet their measurable goals are effective, so control has to do with the establishment and meeting of goals.
- *Internal Process Model*: Effectiveness means the ability to successfully manage the information flow and communications within the firm. Firms able to successfully do this are able to create a stable environment with efficient transfer of necessary information

among constituents. These channels of communication must be established and protected via control.

- *Human Relations Model*: This model is internally focused and regards maintaining a strong constituent culture within the organization. Training and development are emphasized and positive morale is used as a determinant for success. There is cohesion in the workforce and support and belief in the direction of the organization. Without informal control mechanisms to support corporate cultures, this wouldn't be possible.

- *Open Systems Model*: Of course, the ability to grow and continue to acquire resources is key to success. This model addresses an external focus and emphasizes the openness and flexibility required to pursue new goals and new markets. It relies on the ability to adapt to its changing environment and be seen as viable by external organizations. The ability to adapt to gather additional resources can only be done successfully with the right control mechanisms in place.

In further examination of these models, Quinn and Rohrbaugh developed a 2 × 2 matrix, with axis endpoints of flexibility and stability, internal focus, and external focus. For obvious reasons, they address how the basic determinants of success compete with one another. How do we have an internal and external focus; how are we simultaneously flexible and stable? We'll leave that up to the management scholars, but our question regards how do we control this? How do we provide the right mechanisms that allow the achievement of these competing characteristics of success? I am suggesting that there is no perfect control scenario, I guess if there was, we would have experienced the perfect organization by now!

This book considers social control theory, so let's briefly consider the term "social". In a Weberian sense, there is little "social" to control. Everything is efficient, formalized, and impersonal. However, Granovetter (1985) and others are quick to note that all transactions are wrapped in a social context. O'Reilly and Chatman (1996) referred to the social context as a shared, normative order that shapes and guides interpretations of events. This greatly expands our notion of who is doing the controlling, and how. We might consider this social context as relatively weak (e.g., simple everyday norms that guide transactions) or particularly strong (an organizational culture that drives the firm). Either way, control is with us and is worthy of study.

The rules mentioned above are not written without the input of humans and their concern for the impact of the rules on themselves. Remember, economic humans are self-concerned above all else. There is interpretation, based on human bias or error, on how the rules are monitored and observed, and enforcement of rules is not available in every situation. So, despite the messiness of the process, it is necessary for us to consider the non-purely bureaucratic notions of control. Although this is more accurate, it is indeed untidy.

Ellickson (1991) refers to social control as a means of extra-legal dispute resolution among members of a social system with loose social ties. That is, it is a control system that extends beyond legal stipulations within a social network. Janowitz (1975) described social control as the capacity of a society to regulate itself according to desired principles and values. Black (1998) described it as, simply, the handling of right and wrong.

So, what do we know about social control so far? We know that,

- control is a prevalent form of managing transactions within business relationships;
- control monitors how work is done, via two general forms, the performance of appropriate behaviors and the achievement of certain outcomes;
- overall modes of control — how control is manifested — come in informal and formal flavors. One is planned, specific, applied, and interpreted by the book. The informal mode of control is, instead, based on the social dimension of the transaction, is not necessarily

pragmatic, but is grounded in fairness, reciprocity, and the norms of general exchange;

- control is typically performed by one party on the other based on the authority in a contract or hierarchy (i.e., unilateral control, formal control, authority control) or via a mutual understanding of the social aspects of the relationship (i.e., bilateral control, informal control, trust);
- control and the mechanisms of control can be used as independent or dependent variables;
- control may or may not work, depending on the situation.

For our discussion on control, we will limit ourselves to business relationships. We are interested in how organizations with a business motive can manage transactions with other organizations. We are interested in the management tools — control mechanisms — of business organizations as applied to dyadic behavior and more. We will discuss the origins of such mechanisms, how they are applied, and, eventually, the conditions under which they can succeed.

Discussion: Semantics?

Governance, control, coordination … isn't it all just semantics? In a sense, maybe, but a common language is important to any epistemology. A common language helps a field advance and drives similar methodologies and measurement techniques.

It seems that the governance/control semantics have always overlapped. Following Merchant's (1988) description of control, however, it seems necessary to separate the front and back ends of governance. Although monitoring is certainly part of control, it is just that, a portion of the whole. Focusing on a similar understanding of control allows us to understand how setting standards, monitoring, and sanctioning can align for better firm performance.

Thus, how does control differ from governance and other considerations of exchange? Well, it generally depends on which governance theory control is compared to, but in general, if control is the back end, it does not subsume the following:

- Marketing to potential partners, where new relationships are sought;
- Relationship formation, where the parties to the exchange test the beginning of the new relationship;
- Planning, where the parties or the exchange work to organize the next steps to a successful future; and
- Introduction/launch, where the fruits of the new partners' labor have just begun.

Thus, we can see that control is a subset of the total exchange relationship. Control is, indeed, the back end, keeping the exchange on track.

Chapter 2

Overview of the Control Framework

In this chapter, we introduce social control theory and discuss the organization from which control emanates, that is, the controller. In this discussion, after introducing our primary subject of the text, we identify three controllers and examine the differences in control based on the controller. By examining the controller, the target of control, and the rules of control, we examine control in its complete context. We refer to this context as a *system of control*. The system of control considers the controller, the mode of control used by the controller (formal or informal), and the mechanisms used by the controller (setting standards, monitoring, and sanctioning with rewards or punishments). Let us answer the question, "What is social control theory?"

Social Control Theory

Social control theory explains how one actor to an extent determines the activities/outcomes of another actor. It also determines the structure of the relationship between the actors and the chances of positive and negative outcomes of the exchange. Social control theory is described as a meta theory because it is concerned with attempts to make sense of different theories that claim to explain the phenomena within a particular disciplinary domain. In our case, the different

Table 2.1. How Social Control Theory Subsumes the Other Major Governance Theories

Governance Theory	Similarities with Social Control Theory
Transaction Cost Analysis	Control is determined based on calculations of the governance costs of the transaction and changes in the control structure.
Agency	Target's response to control is based on an agent's *ex-ante* and *ex-post* costs. May respond positively or negatively to the contract by considering the costs of monitoring and compliance. Considers reputation effects.
Power/Dependence	Control structure is based on the dependence structure between dyadic actors. Changes in structure change the costs of control.
Contract Theory	Contracts specify the total relationship in terms of setting standards and enforcement. Contracts can be messy and have requisite costs associated with them.
Relational Norms	Social dimension is efficient; can operate with a formal mechanism as well.
Trust Theory	Shared goals motivate trusting relationship; relationship is highly efficient at most times.
Organizational Control	Considers available information and optimal monitoring methods.
Incentive Theory	Incentives are a key element to gaining and keeping control. Also considers control redress.
Stewardship Theory	Shared goals are accommodated.
Governance Theory	Includes the "back end" of the governance process. Overlap of rules of control. Multiple modes.

theories are the basic theories of governance, which are described in Chapter 1. In Table 2.1, we summarize what each theory has in common with social control theory, which is necessary for social control theory to carry the moniker "meta theory."

Definition of social control theory

Social control theory explains how one actor to an extent determines the activities/outcomes of another actor. Social control theory, as discussed here, is derived from social control theory as applied to the fields of anthropology, sociology, law, and economics. In these cases, social control theory is a very broad, very loose theory that describes how groups interact with one another to persuade or convince. Primary settings in this domain include political movements, families, governments, and national concerns such as healthcare and crime. One goal of this book is to more clearly and tightly specify how the theory works, its assumptions, its settings, its definitions, and its axioms. But first, who are the actors that we will examine?

In a business setting, the actors in social control theory are groups, firms, or organizations (including legal entities) that are engaged in interorganizational exchange of some kind. These may take the form of dyadic relationships (buyer–seller, channels of distribution, supply chains), network relationships, or intergroup organizational relationships. In any exchange there is a controller and a target of control. Typically, the controller attempts to instill its control mechanisms on the target. The controller must hold a *license* to control. This license gives the controller the right to exercise some type of authority over its target of control. The license is based in hierarchical authority, contractual authority, power, or industry norms. In certain cases, (such as when there are shared goals) there are multiple controllers/targets to one exchange.

The social control framework

The Mechanisms of Control: There are three broad types of mechanisms that are used to keep a relationship on track. *Setting standards* represents the creation, writing, and maintenance of documents such as contracts, policies, legal documents, and other codified statements that guide the expectations of the relationship. *Monitoring* ensures that standards are checked systematically in terms of examining the behaviors of the target and/or the outputs of the target. These are designed to ensure that the standards are maintained. *Sanctions* enforce the standards by implementing incentives, which are various rewards, motivations, and payments, and finally, punishments, which may include fines, poor assignments, and even firings and exiting the relationship.

The Modes of Control: Control is delivered by the controller using two modes, the formal mode of control and the informal mode of control. In the *formal mode of control*, the rules of control are applied in very specific, rigid, and unambiguous ways. They are delivered, supported, and maintained in a "by the book" fashion. Contracts are strictly followed, updated, and referenced. The monitoring mechanisms are strictly applied and adhered to, and the monitoring data produced determine the sanctions. Sanctions rigidly enforce the standards to reward or punish as specified. The *informal mode of control* represents the social dynamic of the relationship, so the rules of control tend to be applied in a very loose, non-rigid manner. Typically, psychological contracts replace/modify written contracts, thus the agreement becomes one more of expectations and beliefs than codified writings. Informal monitoring is not based on counting outputs and observing behaviors, but more on ensuring that the partners have the same goals in mind and the relationship remains equitable. Informal sanctions include informal incentives, which are longer term in nature (that is, not based on salaries, commissions, and bonuses), and informal punishments where shortcomings and inequitable situations are made up for over time.

The Systems of Control: A *system of control*, of which there are three, refers to the entity that holds the license to control. The first control system is the *self-control system* (also known as first-party control). This refers to control of the organization by the organization. Formal and informal rules are applied to itself. The *dyadic control system* (second-party control) occurs when one party to the dyad controls the target of control by formal and informal rules. Finally, the *third-party control system* exists when an outside party (regulator, trade association, legal organization) controls one or more members of the dyad or network.

Finally, because all economic transactions are wrapped in a social context, some combination of formal and informal controls are applied simultaneously at virtually all times. In social control theory, there are no purely formal or purely informal control relationships. Thus, it should be noted that a control combination exists for each exchange transaction (Ellickson 1987). These combinations consist of systems, mechanisms, and modes. For instance, a regulator (third-party control) may provide an informal warning to a constituent because the constituent was deemed to have violated the formal contract, perhaps a supplier (dyadic control) may establish a new monitoring scheme for a dealer which includes outcome monitoring and informal sanctions. These combinations of control are known as the "structure of the control relationship."

The Emergence of Control

Black (1976) suggests that control is a function of a social breakdown in the fabric of society. Formal control, which is based on the rule of law, emerges to quell chaos and unrest. Formal control provides the necessary information for targets of control to perform as requested, plus it is backed up by some form of authority. Controllers that use formal control are interested in moving from a disorganized situation into one that they command. In a business setting, formal control emerges as an authority-based way to align divergent goals. Firms have broad-reaching guidelines, rules, and directives that state how things are to be done. Although they may or may not be specifically applied, they guide the relationship, nonetheless. For the controller to reach its desired objective, it sometimes must force compliance, because norms may not exist to motivate agreement. This is often achieved via the setting of standards, monitoring, and sanctioning. In a channel setting this amounts to suppliers that employ regional marketing personnel to work closely with dealers and distributors to ensure that the transformation process is supported, in terms of the supplier.

Informal control may emerge for several reasons. First, Ouchi (1979) suggests that when satisfactory monitoring information is unavailable — that is, no outcome or behavioral monitoring information — norms must guide surveillance. This requires an informal unwritten agreement by both organizations as to the appropriate attitudes and actions of their members. Because norms are shared, the controller and the target's goals and desired outcomes are likely similar. Second, if satisfactory formal measures are unavailable over time, norms arise after long periods of trial and error (O'Reilly and Chatman 1996). Third, when dependence on one another is significant and shared — that is high and mutual dependence — organizations tend to develop similar goals and are forced to trust one another. Heide (1994) demonstrated how relational norms tend to emerge in such situations. Fourth, when firms mutually invest in the relationship it is a signal that they are committed to one another in the future for fear of losing their investment hostage (Anderson and Weitz 1992). As both firms are locked into the relationship, similar goals emerge, as do norms of behavior and attitudes. This causes a mutually agreed upon set of control rules. Finally, research suggests that informal controls emerge over time from our closest associates such as family and friends, reference groups, service encounters, and even traditional authority (O'Reilly and Chatman 1996).

License to Control

As in real life, not all can control. For instance, few firms if any are able to dictate terms and conditions to Walmart. Walmart may allow concessions in contracts, but it is at their discretion. Walmart policy dictates that they are not part of a channel, purchasing from the supplier's intermediaries. Instead, they demand to be dealt with directly, causing many suppliers to circumvent their traditional channel in lieu of the opportunity to sell to Walmart. Suppliers that do this are often labeled "channel violators," and may even be boycotted, but for many it is worth it to deal with such a powerful force in the marketplace.

We might surmise that control, then, is a function of size; the larger the firm, the more control is possible. But that is only part of the story because small firms can become market leaders and control their channel, including larger firms in the channel. How?

To control, it is necessary to obtain a license to control. A license to control provides the firm with the ability to have firms allow themselves to be controlled, be it through authority of some kind or agreement. A license may force control via size and other attributes, or it may have control attempts allowed for other reasons. Importantly, licenses are earned in different ways for formal and informal control.

Regarding formal control, the license is a function of the *power* that the controller has over the target of control, which allows the controller to force its way on the target. The target has little option but to acquiesce to control attempts. There are several sources of power (Frazier 1983, French and Raven 1959), which allow the controller to influence the activities and behaviors of the controlled target. The primary sources include:

- *Legitimate Authority:* This is usually available in a contract or other document such as a set of dealer guidelines. The controller may have written clauses into the contract specifying activities that must be performed. If not performed, the controller has the right to rely on legal action to force performance.
- *Reward and Punishment:* Economic man is unlikely to act unless they are rewarded or punished in some way for such actions. Rewards typically include high-powered incentives such as cash, margin increases, bonuses, commission increases, and other monetary-based rewards based on performance. Further, rewards can be taken away, thus monetary-based rewards (loss of commission,

bonuses, margins, etc.) and other punishments might be leveled on the partner.

- *Expertise*: A firm that has a technology advantage, such as Apple with their iPhones, provides targets of control with trust and a desire to work with the controller. Usually, market leaders due to advantages in products or services provide their networks with additional opportunities and higher incomes.

Research indicates that such sources of power lead directly to various types of influence attempts, acquiescence, and (often) market success (Gundlach and Cadotte 1994). Thus, power and authority are the primary forms of license in formal control situations.

Informal control works in a very different way. It is based on the formation of norm-based activities and beliefs that both parties seek similar outcomes. There are two licenses in the use of informal control. Both are available due to the establishment of a clan-based form of governance.

First, there must be *agreement* on the specifications of the work arrangement. This indicates that the target of control recognizes the controller has the expertise to guide the situation and that norms can grow from this agreement. Targets accept control because they want to, not have to, which validates the controllers' position. In our food safety study, we (Gilliland and Manning 2002) found out that agreement with the food safety regulations made it more likely that appropriate behaviors would be followed, and less cheating would occur. When an agreement is not available, informal control cannot be instituted. Second, trust between the parties must be established. This license suggests that it is acceptable for the controller to believe that the target's actions are honest and open, and it suggests that the target of control believes the controller has the expertise necessary to guide its behaviors. What also counts is what comes with trust. Trust drives the presence of relational norms (Das and Teng 2001) and a commitment or bonding of the parties. Other drivers of relational norms include mutual levels of dependence (Heide 1994) and loyalty (Gilliland and Bello 2002). Thus, an informal control license is available via agreement and trust in the other party.

Desired Outcomes of Control

If there is no point to control, controllers would not emerge, they would not employ specific control rules to achieve their goals of controlling one another, and outcomes wouldn't matter. In this section, we will briefly investigate some of the outcomes of control. Fair warning that this is somewhat uncharted ground when it comes to theory development, and it is based largely on an observation of the literature.

Control scholars in their respective fields have used a great number of dependent variables to measure the outcomes of control. However, we must note that such outcomes may not be the intent of the control mechanism implemented but may be a residual effect. Also, we must consider that control — particularly formal control, is generally a choice, and that the particular mechanism would not be implemented unless an intended result was sought.

In our business setting formal control emerges to ensure that all tasks are completed appropriately and that targets of control are performing as specified in the work agreement. This can best be achieved by gaining *compliance* — an organization's willing adherence to requests — from the control targets (Kashyap *et al.* 2012). Thus, when organizations (or individuals) comply they do as requested in terms of task performance, effort, appropriate behavior, and cooperation. This may be due to the power differences between the parties, the legal-backed contract, legitimate authority, or to meet incentive offers. Also, compliance adds to the transaction value of the exchange. *Transaction value* (Kleinaltenkamp *et al.* 2022, Lindgreen *et al.* 2012) is the difference between revenues and costs of the goods and services in the exchange. As compliance increases, performance is as planned, coordination is high, and the transactional portion of the exchange attains a higher value position.

Compliance, however, is a double-edged sword. The other edge being the lack of autonomy experienced by the target that comes with compliance, and the potential for negative feelings and retaliation due to this lack of autonomy. Thus, even though compliance is achieved, retaliation in the form of neglect, cheating, and other opportunistic behaviors may emerge as well.

Part of the existence of shared norms becomes fairness and equity. Based on this logic, Ellickson (1987) suggests that the desired outcome of informal controls is *welfare maximization* of all parties. Welfare maximization is a subjective state based on satisfaction. Thus, the interorganizational literature might say that the desired outcome of informal control is satisfaction. Because control must consider the state of both parties, when satisfaction is maximized on both sides of the dyad, it is as good as it can be, and is hopefully a positive solution to the control problem. Also, because norms are shared, how to go about daily behaviors such as coordinating tasks is mutually understood. Tasks are coordinated due to readily sharing information from both parties. Such task coordination increases the transactional value of the relationship, and maximizing the welfare of all increases the *relational value* of the relationship. Relational value (Kleinaltenkamp *et al.* 2022) concerns the additional value added to the exchange due to the social considerations of the partners.

Discussion: Frameworks

If the objective of a theoretical model is to explain (Hunt 1991), what is the purpose of a framework? The purpose of a framework is to organize and represent a phenomenon. Frameworks, to be helpful to a theorist, must be intersubjectively certifiable (when different researchers with different beliefs and motives obtain the same or similar results) and the model must be empirically testable. Thus, the difference between a framework and a theory is that a theory explains "why," whereas a framework ensures that all the pieces and parts of the model are in the right place.

For a general framework of control, see Chapters 2–5 and Gilliland (2023), where a complex control framework is identified. The remainder of the book will be spent attempting to turn that framework into a theory. To do so, I will rely on standard theory-building tools to form appropriate explanations of how all these parts work together.

Chapter 3

The Modes and Mechanisms of Control

Ferdinand Tönnies was a 19th-century German sociologist and economist. He described a continuum of how people lived in relation to their families, groups, and the state, known as the *Gemeinschaft–Gesellschaft* continuum. Interestingly, he wrote that human behavior existed along this continuum and that someone's place on the continuum could be described by their behaviors. At one end of the continuum, *Gemeinschaft* relationships are based on community and family and an individual's emotional connections. *Gemeinschaft* is German for "community" and reflects Tönnies' thoughts about village and rural life. People tended to have strong social relationships with one another, banded together, and did not require large government direction to guide how they lived. Sports organizations, churches, local clubs, and the general rural existence defined this end of the continuum. *Gesellschaft* refers to "society" and is reflective of life in the big city. Society, not local relationships, controlled behavior via the use of a legal structure, large corporations, and a capitalist economy. The social bonds of family and friends are replaced with scientific rationality, self-interested behaviors, and the efficient coordination of tasks.[1] Although these ideal types are extreme, they reflect the range in which people and groups might be organized (Tönnies [1887] 1957).

Today, inter-organizational relationships are grounded in more than economics. The modern view is that an individual economic transaction most always has a social dimension (Lado *et al.* 2008). This relates particularly well to B2B exchange. As Thomas Bonoma said, "Companies don't buy, people do," and because people are involved, the purchase must consider not only the rational, or *Gesellschaft* dimension of the transaction but the involvement of personal relationships — both positive and negative — that might form. Each transaction can be placed on Tönnies' continuum: some exchanges are highly rational, economic-based, and logical (consider a straight rebuy of a vendor's product from an OEM) and some must struggle to deal with the vastness of the social dimension as well (perhaps forming a joint venture). Okay, but what does this mean for control?

First, in modern society, we are clearly controlled by formal and informal means. Formally, we have a vast legal system that controls what is and what is not a criminal act. A crime is a crime and there are written rules and regulations — some quite extensive, as in anti-trust law — that specify procedures and punishments to fit the crime. There are different classes of felonies and misdemeanors that cover misbehaviors, from murder first-class all the way to petty theft and public intoxication. There are other sets of formal laws and regulations that cover driving offenses, family relations, bankruptcies, small claims, and civil transgressions. Other formal regulations can be found in organizations — business policies, school rules, homeowners association bylaws, club charters — and in individual relationships — marriage contracts, real-estate transactions, and personal lawsuits.

---

[1] It may be useful to note that Max Weber based many of his thoughts and writings on Tönnies' notion of *Gesellschaft*, in determining that ideal corporations should be rational, logical, hierarchical, and efficient.

One thing formal controls have in common is that they are usually codified in some way.

Although our lives are structured by formal controls, we often rely on the *Gemeinschaft* dimension when considering how to behave on an everyday basis. When considering issues of control, *Gemeinschaft* refers to control via informal mechanisms, such as learning from peers, relational exchange, and the establishment of everyday norms — even though they may seem irrational — to guide transactions.

Informal controls are more complex than formal controls because they are not written, they often change, they are usually invisible, they are determined by unofficial groups and organizations, and they do not come with clear sanctions. I list four considerations when working with informal control.

- *Informal control is generally based on a positive relationship*: Families deciding on vacations, political organizations working with constituents, friends choosing what film to attend, football teams determining strategies for the second half, are all controlled by themselves, or a member of the group (the coach or captain). When members of the group have similar beliefs, goals, and intentions, they are willing to cede personal autonomy and power for the good of the group. Relational norms and expectations arise on which they all agree (the captain is our leader), and control proceeds.
- *Informal control is often based on everyday norms*: Everyday norms guide behaviors, but are not necessarily based in strong social relationships; rather, they can be a function of "doing things the way they've always been done." Everyday norms cover what we wear to work vs. what we wear to the beach, the language we use at the bar vs. the language we use during board meetings, and so on. One thing to understand about everyday norms, they are not necessarily positive. The everyday norms of English football hooligans was to tear up pubs, shops, and everything else in the opponents' community. Mostly, however, everyday norms reflect the best way

to get things done, often while circumventing formal rules or requirements.

- *Informal control includes interpretations of formal control*: Clearly, not everyone follows formal guidelines. For instance, we speed and sometimes we get caught. From the traffic cops' perspective, they can apply the rule and write us a ticket for going 56 in a 55 zone, or they can let us off with a lecture for going 65 in that same zone. Thus, informal control includes choosing *whether* and *how* to apply formal mechanisms. In our earlier example, some food inspectors let their clients go with education about the necessity of the rule and a bit of training. Gary Bell, whom we met in the Introduction, throws his dealer contracts into a file drawer. Thus, where we lie on the *Gemeinschaft–Gesellschaft* continuum may be a function of individual rule interpretation.

- *Informal control is grounded in our personal beliefs and ethics*: Because we all have different ethical guidelines, we interpret formal controls and how they're applied in different ways. Should those that commit a crime have the book thrown at them, or are they worthy of a reduced sentence? Likewise, we apply our ethics and beliefs to political situations — are those that avoid the draft political protestors or draft dodgers — and other aspects of daily life.

Of course, as with the original concepts of *Gesellschaft* and *Gemeinschaft*, formal and informal controls are ideal types. They describe an unreal situation where one dimension is in existence and the other is not. Clearly, we use combinations of control modes (which will become an important theme in this book). We don't wear our swimsuits to meetings at work, but sometimes people may show up in workout clothes. The state patrolman who let you off on the speeding ticket might have also given you a formal warning or at least lectured you on the formal speed limit. We will see these combinations of control modes in business relationships as well. In fact, now that we have established the foundation of control, we should be getting a feel for how complex control — particularly informal control — can be. Let's proceed by looking at how formal and informal controls oversee business relationships.

Formal and Informal Modes of Control in Business Relationships

The modes of control are framed by Tönnies' notions of community and are found in a wide range of governance and organizational control theories, as discussed previously. Formal control is the basis for understanding TCA, agency, and other governance theories. Informal control derives primarily from relational norms. Formal control is based on rationality and logic and has a goal of stability of the business relationship and economic efficiency of the exchange. Informal control is more interested in social factors of the exchange and shared understandings. A summary comparison of formal and informal control is offered in Table 3.1.

The formal mode of control of business relationships

Virtually every business relationship has a formal dimension. Imagine entering a business relationship, even with a friend, without some form of a contract. Formal control requirements are typically found in a contract that is rational and impersonal and supported by a legal system (Hechter 1987). Formal control is designed to be written, monitored, and enforced. It is expected that it will be interpreted by the book. In the literature, formal controls have been identified in different ways, depending on the theory from which they emanate. For instance, formal control is the legitimate authority established in a written contract (Lusch and Brown 1996) or in an authoritative relationship (Rubin 1990). It is the use of power in a coercive way (threat or reward influence strategies; Frazier 1984, Gundlach and Cadotte 1994). Formal control is the use of bureaucratic monitoring

Table 3.1. Formal vs. Informal Control across Control Systems

	Formal Control Mode	Informal Control Mode
Bases for Existence	*Impersonal* relationships: Logical and rational thinking, calculative assessment, instrumental reasoning	*Organic* relationships: Norms of understanding and behavior, affect, relational assessment
Controllers		
Self-Control System	The actor follows instrumental and self-interested motivations to control its actions. A calculative assessment of its gains and losses is based on established company bylaws and codes of conduct, rules, laws, and formalized procedures	The actor is driven to make everyday decisions based on a general principle of benevolence toward others, moral principles, and the welfare of the greatest good. Also, managers are driven by their own moral and ethical beliefs in determining the firm's way forward
	Setting Standards: Firm codes and guidelines, mission statements	*Setting Standards*: Psychological contract between firms and employees, moral and ethical codes
	Monitoring: Performance reviews, reviews of financial performance	*Monitoring*: Self-assessment
	Sanctioning: Promotions and demotions, bonuses, firings	*Sanctioning*: Identification, ostracism, threats, shunning behaviors
Dyadic Control System	Transactions of a short- or medium-term horizon. Bureaucratic, unilateral control driven by carefully specified contracts and power advantages	Personal and relational bonds between two parties, daily interaction is a function of two-way communication, agreed upon modifications to plans, and mutually understood strategies and tactics. The written contract is seldom used in lieu of relational norms and understandings

	Setting Standards: Simple and complex contracts and agreements *Monitoring*: Outcome and process monitoring *Sanctioning*: High-powered incentives, compensatory sanctions	*Setting Standards*: Informal or bilateral understandings *Monitoring*: Goal monitoring *Sanctioning*: Low-powered incentives, therapeutic and conciliatory sanctions
Third Party Control System	Company rules, legal decisions. The legal system is enacted in terms of regulatory bodies or courts of law. Strict legal and regulatory guidelines are delivered and imposed on the partners *Setting Standards*: Business law, trade association rules, regulatory rules *Monitoring*: Discovery, inspection *Sanctioning*: Judicial decisions, direct regulatory sanctions	Trade associations, industry groups, consultants, and others seek to return actions of the firm to those as prescribed by industry norms *Setting Standards*: Informal guidelines required by normative institutions (e.g., trade associations) and acceptable public norms and expectations *Monitoring*: Reporting as required by normative institutions, observance of public opinion *Sanctioning*: Discussion, cajoling, indirect regulatory sanctions

mechanisms (Ouchi 1979), monetary incentives (Blattberg and Neslin 1990), and other unilateral governance processes (Heide 1994).

Even contracts that aren't referred to on a regular basis still structure the relationship. On a smaller scale, dealers and distributors are constrained to specific behaviors and activities to comply with their suppliers' desires. For instance, a large Italian firm marketing woodworking machinery to small businesses and hobbyists requires every sales rep at their dealer locations to have no more than 500 customers. It is a formal requirement supported by the contract. Corporate guidelines, business law, and antitrust regulations also control relationships. Questions regarding formal requirements, rules, laws, and guidelines are interpreted logically, rationally, and bureaucratically. However, despite their required existence, formal controls are often seen as coercive, intrusive, and inefficient (Heide *et al.* 2007, Kumar *et al.* 2011) because the forcing of specific behaviors and procedures often results in backlash, resentment, and loss of autonomy.

The informal mode of control of business relationships

Robert Ellickson, a legal scholar who wrote on the combinations of law and informal control, finds that law has its limitations, and goes so far as to say that "In many contexts, law is not central to the maintenance of social order" (1991, p. 280). Imagine if a neighbor's cows broke down the fence surrounding your farm, doing damage. There are two avenues of recourse: legal or informal. Ellickson describes that law has a cost of implementation. That is, as a farmer, you must find out how the legal system works (possibly by hiring an expensive attorney), how to file suit, the language of the law, and how to ask for compensation. Then, you must wait months before a judgment is passed, which you may or may not agree with. Finally, damage may be done to a previously working relationship, which has its own set of costs. In his in-depth study of farmers' boundaries between neighbors, Ellickson found that "people are aware that the legal system is a relatively costly system of dispute resolution and therefore often choose to turn a deaf ear to it" (p. 281). For this reason, informal control in business relationships must be considered.

Informal relationships are juxtaposed with the formal mode of control. Informal control is "tinged with affect" and emotion and takes traditional and existing behavioral norms into account (Hechter 1987, p. 21). Such relationships consider non-legal bonds and commitments, and parties may suppress their self-interest for the good of the collective whole. While formal control structures relationships between organizations, informal control supplements the structure, fill in holes in incomplete contracts, determines how formal controls are interpreted and used, and may even establish the everyday norms of how the relationship works. These informal controls are typically based on everyday exchange routines and norms, and consider workers' individual beliefs, firms, competitors, and industry members — including government regulators and industry trade associations (Shapiro 1987).

The informal mode of control might be thought of as based on the social relationship (Rokkan *et al.* 2003, Kumar *et al.* 2011). The degree of the informal aspect of any social business relationship might vary from large (shared relational norms and expectations of long-term orientation; Ganesan 1994, Ring and Van de Ven 1994) to basic norm-sharing based on typical ways of conducting business. Informal controls in business settings include relational norms of flexibility, solidarity, mutual decision-making, and proprietary information sharing (Heide and John 1992); clan control (Ouchi 1979); bilateral governance mechanisms (Heide 1994); low-powered or non-instrumental incentives (Obadia *et al.* 2015); and everyday norms of behavior (Gilliland 2023).

However, Ellickson finds there are limits to informal controls just as there are with formal controls. Primarily, when informal control is implemented, there is no guarantee that the adversaries will receive the distributive or corrective judgment that they might believe is fair, or that the legal system might reward. Second, there is no enforcement built in to when and how, or even how much, is paid in compensation. Finally, informal controls are based on people, and when people in the group change or become more distant from one another, the agreement may change or break down.

The Mechanisms of Control

For a moment, imagine an industrial lighting distribution channel where there is plenty of work to be done. When a new building is built the lights must be specified by an architect, lighting engineer, or design-build contractor. The lighting spec must be put out to bid and a chosen supplier selected. The accompanying wiring and controls must be designed by the supplier. The design must be approved by the owner, fire marshal, contractor, and others. The supplier's lights must be manufactured, stocked, and eventually shipped to the job site. They must be properly installed and checked. Who controls this situation, and what mechanisms does the controller use to accomplish the work that is required to make for a successful installation?

In this industry, the lighting supplier generally controls the overall situation. Now, the question becomes, "How is the process managed; how is the work of the channel accomplished?" Since the 1960s, research has delved into how a controller implements the mechanisms of control that ensure the processes are satisfactorily accomplished. I recently summarized a lot of this research and suggested that controlling organizations were responsible for instituting three types of mechanisms that must be successfully accomplished to control another (Gilliland 2023).

Setting standards

The first mechanism is setting standards. Setting standards involves identifying and communicating the things that must be done to accomplish the specific tasks needed to move the relationship forward. In a lighting channel, these might include quality and speed of manufacture, logistical goals and guidelines, and installation and testing procedures. Importantly, setting standards identifies the specific conduct that is measured, assessed, and sanctioned (rewarded or punished), in some way. Standards might be established formally or informally. As you would expect, the formal setting of standards might include written guidelines and contracts, which tell how to do things, and the expectations of what is to be accomplished. Clear measurement standards are often set to keep an eye on the overall satisfaction of the clients. The informal setting of standards can be thought of as expectations of what should be accomplished. For instance, a formal standard for the success of a lighting agent or distributor might be monthly revenue. But what if the economy is poor and a strong competitor has entered the market? Informal standards might, in this case, modify the formal requirements to a more realistic set of numbers.

Monitoring

The second mechanism is monitoring. Once standards are set, they must be checked. Monitoring is a common component of governance across most all theoretic depictions of control. Ouchi (1979) provides an excellent early description of monitoring. Formal monitoring has been identified by Ouchi and others as a way to judge success. There are two general types of formal monitoring. *Outcome monitoring* can be described as the counting of things that were established in the first mechanism. How many units shipped, what is market penetration, what is customer satisfaction, what are the food holding temperatures, etc.? However, although outcome monitoring describes *how many*, it does not describe *how*. This is attainable via behavioral monitoring. *Behavioral monitoring* includes observing, confirming, or correcting how things are done. Popular in the marketing sales literature, behavioral monitoring describes the salesperson's execution of the selling process. If formal monitoring is not available or satisfactory (perhaps the organization is monitoring the wrong things), *goal monitoring* is the informal form of monitoring (Gilliland *et al.* 2010). Known also as "clan control," goal monitoring is the consideration of how members of a group conform to informal norms. It is the checking of whether group members adequately share norm-based goals.

Sanctioning

The third mechanism is sanctioning. Sanctioning can be described as correction mechanisms that ensure that rewards or punishments are distributed based on whether behaviors or outcomes do not meet pre-established standards (as determined by the monitoring mechanisms). Sanctioning is quite complex and uses various incentive forms to reward those that meet or exceed goals and various punishments or reprimands for those that do not. Formal sanctioning includes high-powered incentives (Williamson 1991), which can be thought of as immediate payments for accomplishing specified tasks. Sales commissions, salaries, bonuses, and other rewards link performance directly to pay, and are particularly motivating. These are also known as extrinsic incentives (Benabou and Tirole 2003). Regarding formal punishments, contractual enforcements may specify what happens in the contract or in a judicial decision (firings, reduction in bonuses or commissions, etc.).

Informal sanctioning occurs, again based on the norms of the relationship. Informal sanctions include incentives such as low-powered incentives (incentives that are awarded over time and are not as tightly aligned with motivation and performance). Low-powered, or intrinsic incentives, may include 401(k)s, health insurance, training programs, and other forms of support (see Gilliland 2003). Finally, informal punishments may include cajoling, indirect regulatory sanctions, ostracism, and threats of termination.

Codification

Formal controls are most always codified in some way, either through official contracts, corporate positioning policy statements, codes of conduct, 10-K reports, annual reports, or in letters and notes to employees. These serve as official guidelines and directives for processes and behaviors that drive firms, organizations, and relationships between firms. However, due to the costs of writing contracts and our inability to predict the future, most all contracts and written communications are incomplete. Because contracts are a set of promises that commit one to future action (Farnsworth 1982), much of the future becomes undefined as to what actions are appropriate to perform. This is where an informal set of usually unwritten norms and directives appears. Known as the psychological contract, it describes a belief regarding an obligation (promise), based on performance or expected performance (Rousseau 1989). The psychological contract, depending on its breadth, fills in the holes between the stipulations in written documentation.

From where does the psychological contract emanate? From norms that emerge between the parties. Thus, norms — unwritten beliefs — drive a great deal of the activities between people, organizations, and firms. Imagine working with a very incomplete contract and the lack of established norms of behavior. Chaos, or at least confusion, would ensue. Thus, it is believed that the informal contract — the non-codified set of agreements — completes and complements the formal contract, allowing the working of important tasks.

The problem with this is that norms, because they are unwritten, are not seen equally by all parties (Robinson and Rousseau 1994). In fact, Weiner (1988) describes norms as an "ought," stating that they define behaviors. Thus, as norms change, the expectation of behaviors change. For example, imagine a firm offering a 10% wage increase that has been constant for several years. Thus, on the part of the employees a norm might emerge that they receive 10% raises each year. However, management might interpret the 10% increase not as a promise, but as a pure function of revenues, costs, and expected future performance; it may not share in the psychological contract.

Does Control Work?

There are many ways to address this question, but I first want to note that control *must* work. Without control, as a society we are doomed, and as businesses we stand little chance of success. All we need do is look around us and we find so many examples of successfully designed and implemented control strategies, suggesting control must and does work. However, in other cases, control has been found to increase opportunistic behaviors (Oliviera and Lumineau 2019), shirking (Gilliland and Kim 2014), hostility (Kaufmann and Stern 1988), conflict (Geyskens *et al.* 1999), poor attitudes (O'Reilly 1989), and risk (Das and Teng 2001). So, it isn't a matter of *if* control works, it is a matter of *when* control works. Another issue that makes it difficult for control to work is the often-unintended outcomes of control. That is, control may work as designed, but there may be residual effects on other aspects of the relationship.

Jaworski (1988) took on the notion of control by examining the effects of the environment on control, and control on the consequences of performance. He suggested that there must be a fit, or match, between the existing environmental conditions on which control is applied, and the control mechanism in use. This book also takes that perspective. There must be some form of match in order to make control work.

Two questions emerge. First, what are the outcomes that are needed for one to claim that control works? Second, what do we mean by "match," or "fit"?

Outcomes required for a successful control implementation include compliance, welfare maximization for all parties, and an increase in (or, at least not a loss of) transactional and relational value. This is a short but difficult-to-achieve list. One reason it is difficult to achieve is because of the competing values framework discussed in Chapter 1 (Quinn and Rohrbaugh 1983). An increase in one dimension of high performance is automatically, or almost automatically, associated with a decrease in another dimension. For instance, stability and flexibility are difficult to achieve simultaneously.

Given this, what is required for the adequate fit between the situation that demands control and the implemented control mechanisms? That is, what must be present, despite the actual control mechanisms and situation, for control to work.

- First, a license to control must be present. The controller must be seen as legitimate in the eyes of the target. This allows trust in the relationship, which drives the process forward. The target must feel that the controller has the ability to complete the control process (force compliance) in terms of making good on contractual promises of sanctions.
- Second, information provided through the interaction between the controller and the target of control must be present. Gilliland and Manning (2002) found that the more information was made available to act on by both parties to control attempts, the more successful was the control. Information is a vital source of any transaction, and a lack of information adds risk and uncertainty to the situation, making control difficult.
- Third, for control to truly be successful, residual effects must be minimized. The control literature is full of unintended consequences. For instance, seemingly successful formal control attempts are often followed by hostility, retaliation, or other opportunistic behaviors (Scheer *et al.* 2003).

Expectations that control will result in the best possible outcomes for both parties also motivate success. Ellickson's (1987) requirement for welfare maximization (which read as satisfaction) for both parties means there is no need for hostility or retaliation, thus reducing the chance of unintended consequences.

Why formal control often does not work

It isn't that formal control *per se* does not work; rather, it is the specific mechanisms of formal control that may fail to produce intended outcomes. We focus on three such mechanisms, incentives, monitoring, and enforcing the contract.

Incentives are very imperfect motivating mechanisms. The target of control is motivated to change its goals in order to earn controller-provided income and other advantages. Unfortunately, incentives only reward visible and difficult-to-measure tasks — much of a reseller's job is hidden from view — and this invites gaming of the system as the target of control will only perform the portion of the job that provides it income. Regarding other mechanisms of formal control, such as monitoring and contract enforcement, the outcomes, while still unintended, are a bit more accessible. Regarding monitoring, retaliation often occurs because there is a loss of autonomy on the part of the controlled (Bijlsma-Frankema and Costa 2005). Outputs or behaviors or both are dictated and surveilled by the controller, and often sanctioned for a failure to perform as required. Even though the target may benefit from the sanctions, it still may take them off track of their own goal sets. Imagine a reseller with a high-quality, high-price position selling a discounted product. If it doesn't fit the corporate strategy it can be detrimental to the distribution relationship. Regarding contract enforcement, this often fails from the perspective of the controller and the target because it is expensive to apply and results may seem arbitrary and unfair (Ellickson 1987). When such enforcement is inappropriately applied, the mechanism may be compromised and lead to reduced adaptations, exploitation, and other harmful behaviors (Caldwell and O'Reilly 1990).

Why informal control often does not work

There is an assumption in the literature that informal control is more effective than formal control in leading to positive control outcomes. It may be. Parties work together to address unique situations and produce effective solutions. They are not bound by expensive control systems such as the law, and contracts that may or may not address their specific needs.

Thus, much less is known about informal control and its failures. Our notion of fit addressed earlier certainly applies to informal incentives (long term and not necessarily cash; Obadia *et al.* 2015), as does recent work in the management field. As a firm or partnership extends its horizon to the longer term, it needs adequate control sanctions — in the form of incentives — to support the motivation of the parties throughout the relationship.

Thus, informal controls are quite successful, but there are issues. First, there can be a clash of personal norms and values with the corporate culture of the firm. Firms have specific and unique cultures, many of which have taken years to cultivate, and the culture may not fit the requirements of individuals within the group. Likewise, corporate mergers and acquisitions are asked to merge possibly dissimilar cultures. We may wonder about the possibility of internal misunderstandings and disagreements between Tata Motors, the low-cost automobile manufacturer from India, and Jaguar-Land Rover, the luxury auto brands out of the UK. However, Tata bought the British brands in 2008 and it has been successful in its management strategies. Just as harmful might be a weak social culture, that is, a lack of commonly understood norms to guide behaviors and attitudes (O'Reilly and Chatman 1996). Without a substantive culture to oversee behaviors, only formal control is left, reducing the probability of a successful fit. In Tata's case, they work hard to separate the brands and allow them to keep their own identities.

If we stretch our thinking a bit and consider trust as a governance, or informal control mechanism (Doney and Cannon 1996),

Lumineau (2017) suggests an interesting situation. As firms trust each other, informal mechanisms take over from formal as the cultural similarities of the firms become more similar and the firms become more willing to accept risk. However, at the same time, part of the relinquishing of formal control means that firms may drop their guard and be less diligent in formal monitoring and oversight. Unfortunately, when the guard drops, a firm can be blindsided by opportunistic behaviors from the other party. Does this happen frequently? I hope not, but it is always a risk.

In summary, a fit between environmental and organizational situations, and the specific mechanisms of control make it difficult for control to work in broad settings. Fortunately, as we will discuss subsequently, a plethora of control mechanisms, formal and informal, exist to bring agreement between parties and successful control opportunities.

Combinations of Control Modes

Like formal and informal controls in society, we must consider how they work together in business relationships. Are they independent of one another? Do they combine in some way? Early investigations were conducted by Jaworski *et al.* (1993). They introduced the notion of primary and secondary controls and suggested that there may be instances where a firm might be characterized as having reliance on different control types, one more prominent than the other. They found the existence of four control combinations:

- *Low Control System*: Where only minor amounts of formal and informal control are used. This might be the case of a transactional relationship, where little defines the exchange from either a formal or informal standpoint.
- *Bureaucratic System*: Significant levels of formal controls — in terms of output and behavioral monitoring — and few informal controls were found. A bureaucratic system can be guided by a contractual relationship or by higher levels of authority.

- *Clan System*: A system with high levels of informal controls and low levels of formal controls. Firms exist in a clan system when guidance is dominated by corporate culture, there is a lack of specific rules, and a high level of collegiality.
- *High Control System*: This system of control is characterized by the heavy use of formal rules, written contracts, and specific regulations, along with heavy use of informal controls, characterized by mutual agreements. We might speculate that this system revolves around a very large and complex relationship, possibly a joint venture.

So, in which direction do we turn? According to Ellickson, control — formal or informal — is implemented based on cost. If informal control is applied more cheaply, it has the chance of returning a better result for the cost of implementation. In fact, in Gilliland (2023), I suggest that as members of a group get closer (less social distance), the costs of executing business transactions decrease, and it becomes easier to implement social controls. But what about "big business" transactions? Let's say two independent cattle companies experience the same problem discussed earlier in the chapter, a group of rogue cows tears through a boundary fence and does damage. Which is more costly, formal or informal control? It's probably easier to get your corporate lawyer, well-versed in cattle liability, to file suit (and likely settle out of court) than it would be for the two firms to make friends — informal control takes time and resources to develop — and eventually work things out.

Discussion: Why Don't We Know More about Social Control?

Social control in business relationships is an elusive topic of which we know far too little. Why is that, especially when we consider Tönnies' work from 150 years ago? There are three primary reasons we struggle with social control.

First, social control derives from a very broad set of literature. The control of organizations, people, and organisms is not from a single body of literature. For answers, social control researchers must glean from economics, anthropology, political economy, sociology, and even the physical sciences such as biology. Plus, recently the business sciences have weighed in, including marketing, management, supply chain, accounting, and more. Not only does this make it hard for the science of social control to agree to and coalesce around a few important topics but it has also prevented an epistemology from developing. This includes agreement on a common set of methodologies to drive the domain forward.

Second, from a business perspective, there are too many competing theories, most with a much further developed vocabulary, set of methodologies, and accepted nomologies. With such commonality it is much easier to advance extant theories, learn from related theories (as stewardship scholars and agency scholars advance their fields), and move forward. Why risk your career on an unspecified area of governance as opposed to a well-specified one (e.g., TCA, agency)?

Third, our topics of study are simply too broad to clearly define them, establish a nomology, and develop methods. Social control in business situations involves virtually every form of social control mode and system. In fact, we might ask the question, "What is *not* considered to be within the domain of social control?" This clearly makes it hard to develop a unifying theory. But the establishment and description of various frameworks is a good place to start.

In summary, business control scholars have a broad handle on governance, administration, and the rules of authority, but without agreed-upon unifying theories it is difficult. An organized, concerted effort should be made to motivate our search for control-based answers to problems of governance.

Chapter 4

The Self-Control System

In this chapter, we continue building our framework for understanding control by introducing the first of the three control systems, the self-control system. The self-control system concerns how an organization controls itself, and how this self-control can be very influential on the control of other organizations and firms. First, before delving into the main topic of the chapter, I discuss self-help, a quite simple concept with very important implications for control of any form. This allows us to move from the individual as the unit of analysis to the firm. Second, I will introduce the control system. We will find that there are three, and that they embody the heart of the book.

Self-Help

Self-help is the genesis of social control. Many anthropologists and sociologists spend their careers studying how people and societies control(led) one another. The key to self-control, historically and in the present day, is a natural phenomenon known as self-help. Self-help is one of the five major forms of conflict management (the others being avoidance, negotiation, settlement, and toleration) and is how individuals commit themselves to social control. That is, it all starts with one individual handling a grievance or difference of opinion with another (Black 1998).

Self-help has been conceptualized as everything from expressing an opinion to committing serious crimes including murder. Murder? What does that have to do with social control? Most forms of murder are committed against acquaintances, friends, or family members. Even though it is certainly a crime, it can also be seen as fair compensation for a wrongdoing or other grievance. Families and others throughout history into the present day often act in retaliation for perceived wrongs and take matters into their own hands to level the score. Crime is also thought of as a rational form of self-help because it is often easier than suing or calling the police, and because it could even be seen as moralistic when crime is committed against bad guys (Black 1998).

Our interest in self-help isn't quite so dreadful. Self-help is committing an act of influence, a grievance, or attempted conflict management toward another. This act may include business-related attempts to control situations, both within and outside of the actor's organization. Greenberger and Strasser (1986) contend that control occurs when people realize their behaviors are independent of desired outcomes. This realization becomes the first step in self-help. Further, this helps fulfill an employee's general need for control in an organization, and, if successful, increases their intrinsic motivation to do a good job. Importantly, as we will discuss subsequently, self-help leads to self-control, which is a key element in understanding individuals' motivation for work.

When a purchasing agent wants to control the price of a purchased product, she may contact the sales rep individually to complain. Picking up the phone and talking to the sales rep is nothing more than self-help in a business environment. Again, not as shocking as committing violent crimes, but conceptually the same. Thus, business-to-business exchange is actually many people attempting self-help on their contemporaries across the dyad.

It is also important to know that the genesis of organizational control is the individual. One person generally gets the control ball rolling — be it formal or informal control — and others within the organization align, or not, with the individual. Thus, organizational control begins with individual self-help.

Related to self-help is the notion of self-motivation. Motivation is vitally important to control as firms seek ways to make employees happier, more productive, and less likely to leave. Motivation explains what gets employees up in the morning and can be used to shape role specifications on the job. It can also be used to design incentive plans — if a firm understands how employees are motivated, it can structure a payment/reward system that compels desired activities.

Theories of motivation

Importantly, factors external to the self may affect self-motivation, a key to self-help. Manz (1986) finds that the formal structure of the organization as well as its informal organizational culture might change employees' self-perceptions of themselves in the organization. Further, standards, rules, policies, and procedures shape employee behaviors, for good or bad, as do the reward and punishment system (which we refer to as "sanctions"). Regarding the primary modern self-motivation theories:

- *Expectancy theory* (Vroom 1964) is based on individuals' expectations that acting in a certain way will result in a desired outcome and that the outcome will have a particular level of attractiveness. The more likely acting in a certain way will return positive outcomes (generally rewards of some kind such as money, esteem, etc.) the more likely that behavior is to be expected. Expectancy theory consists of three general components. *Valence* is the affective orientation that people have regarding a particular outcome. Both positively and negatively (the probability of being ostracized) valenced outcomes can be considered. *Instrumentality* is the strength of the worker's belief that a certain level of work effort will produce a certain outcome. *Expectancy* is the belief that a certain level of effort will provide a desired level of performance. In summary, expectancy theory suggests work effort is a function of the likelihood of success of various outcomes and an individual's affinity for the outcome.

- *Equity theory* (Adams and Freedman 1976) compares employee beliefs in the relationship between their inputs into the job and the outcomes it produces. Thus, if employees feels that they are undercompensated they can change their behaviors in a variety of ways (reduce effort, ask their boss for a raise). The key to equity theory is the employees feelings of justice, that is, the degree of fairness as determined by the amount of the reward (distributive justice), how the reward was determined (procedural justice), and the extent they felt they were treated respectfully (interactional justice).
- *Goal-setting theory* (Locke and Latham 1990) explains how workers' individual goals result in motivation. More specifically, employees work to achieve internal and external goals and those goals will have a degree of difficulty and a high valence. They also know which behaviors will lead to goal accomplishment. Thus, they understand the linkage between goal-setting, effort, and reward of some type. As goals are set and achieved, motivation will increase. Thus, the difficulty of goals can produce work outcomes.
- *Organizational commitment theory* (Allen and Meyer 1996, O'Reilly and Chatman 1996) posits that motivation is a function of how committed workers are to their organization. There are two forms of organizational commitment theory, both of which have achieved empirical support. First, the O'Reilly and Chatman approach suggests three dimensions of employee commitment to an organization: the extent the employee identifies with the roles and activities of the organization (*identification*), the extent they internalize the values of the organization (*internalization*), and the extent they comply (*compliance*). The Allen and Meyer approach also works with

three distinct dimensions of commitment. They suggest that commitment consists of an *affective* dimension (the extent the employee is attached to the organization due to his positive emotions about the organization; a liking), a *calculative* dimension (the extent that the employee is attached due to his economic need to stay with the organization), and a *moral obligation* dimension (the extent that the attachment is due to a feeling that the employee should maintain its affiliation with the organization because it is the right thing to do).

- *Cognitive evaluation theory* (Deci *et al.* 1999) regards intrinsic vs. extrinsic motivation. It suggests that external factors such as monetary rewards, monitoring, and evaluation have a negative impact on a worker's intrinsic motivation to work. In fact, they are thought to "turn" the motivation from an intrinsic one to extrinsic motivation. This is harmful because those with intrinsic motivation perform better, work harder, are happier, and have a longer-term intention of staying. Also, cognitive evaluation theory finds that as feelings of competence and autonomy grow, performance increases.

- *Self-determination theory* (Deci and Ryan 1980, 2000) also focuses on intrinsic and extrinsic motivation and, again, the importance of autonomy for an employee. As feelings of autonomy increase so too does intrinsic motivation. Other factors are also important for intrinsic motivation: competence and relatedness, the feelings of involvement with the organization.

In reviewing these motivation theories we may understand that (1) intrinsic motivation is preferential to extrinsic motivation, (2) there is generally an identification or "liking" of an organization that is necessary to maximize motivation, and (3) autonomy counts. From our control-centric perspective, all of the above are important, but what may be most concerning is that control reduces autonomy in workers. This means that there will be pushback or retaliation of some form against formally implemented control. We will begin to see how that affects performance over the next several chapters. Let us now move from understanding individuals from a motivation and self-help perspective to understanding the self-control system.

The Self-Control System

The self-control system regards how an organization controls itself. Self-control is the easiest of the three control systems to implement and manage because it requires little or no outside consideration. Decisions are made based on internal requirements and can change from time to time, although deliberately, as the organization changes or negotiates new environments, competitors, and other outside interventions.

The guidelines and norms established in self-control guide the organization's conduct, behaviors, and ethics. We will find considerable social-based control in the self-control system as the organization extends beyond its contracts and other formal agreements.

General considerations for self-control

The objectives of self-control help ensure fair treatment of employees and outside partners, smooth operations, and success in the market. *Alignment* is pursued to make sure the firm follows its own objectives regarding its place in the market, its distribution channel, and how employees are treated. Alignment can be checked and modified to meet the requirements of employees, supply and distribution partners, customers, and even competitors (O'Reilly and Chatman 1996). *Motivation* ensures that employees and suborganizations are ready and willing to come to work every day and perform as required. Motivation can be modified to meet changing requirements to ensure employees receive adequate compensation and benefits to move the firm successfully through its environment. Motivation is quite complicated and controversial as we shall see, but without ample motivation employees are not likely to support the organization's goals (Ryan and Deci 2000). *Ethical conduct* ensures that the organization follows both external and internal requirements and expectations for the treatment of employees and others. Considerations for ethical conduct ensure the organization is in compliance with ethical and legal standards and avoids internal and external corruption and deviant behaviors (Lange 2008). Finally, *living up to expectations* includes the promotion and execution of activities and requirements to give external contacts and internal personnel confidence in the ability and stability of the organization, making it safe to do business with (O'Reilly 1989). The application of standards to itself, as well as its ability to self-monitor and self-sanction allow the firm to maintain a delicate balance between itself, its networks, and its environment (Manz 1986).

Like the other systems of control, self-control comes in two modes, the formal mode and the informal mode. Also, self-control follows three standard mechanisms of control, setting standards, monitoring, and sanctioning via incentives and punishments.

The formal mode of self-control

The formal mode of self-control is based on a logical economic calculus of revenues and costs to determine organizational success. Formal self-control involves the processes and procedures developed to get employees to perform and conform to the organization's strategy and position (Schleicher *et al.* 2018). Elements such as customer satisfaction, quality of production, and employee ratings of performance are also measured (but of course, not free of error) and are objective measures of success (Carter 2000, Gibbs 1989). Upper and middle management of the organization derives and measures inputs and outputs to encourage compliance with standards.

Setting Standards: The setting of standards includes identifying and communicating the specific conduct that is rewarded, sanctioned, or left alone (Gilliland 2023). That is, not every specification is formally or informally monitored, even though they help set the expectations of the organization. Written and formally communicated standards guide actions within the organization and boundary spanners' actions at the intersection of business with outside organizations. The standards are manifest in official publications and websites of the firm including human resource policies and rules, mission statements, departmental rules, codes of conduct, travel regulations, employee fraternization policies, remote work regulations, employee goal-setting, and other codified sources of information.

Monitoring: Formal monitoring generally comes in two forms: output monitoring and behavioral monitoring. Output monitoring is the basic counting of agreed-upon outcomes. Sales dollars, market share, territory penetration, units sold, production units rejected, hours clocked-in, inventory control measures, production costs and lead times, and many more ways of keeping track of outputs are systematically recorded and reported on a regular basis. Behavioral monitoring concerns ongoing measures of the processes used by employees, usually in the production and selling functions (Ouchi and Maguire 1975). Behavioral monitoring has been found to be particularly successful in channel and retail situations where the transformation process, the process used to sell, can be easily identified, trained, and performed. A problem with behavioral monitoring is that it can be subjective in nature, while output monitoring tends to be objective (Conroy and Gupta 2016). Further research has suggested that output monitoring can be subject to *criterion deficiency*, where actual and accurate measures are only available for a limited set of tasks. Meanwhile, behavioral monitoring may suffer from *criterion contamination*, where extraneous factors are filtered into the evaluation (Conroy and Gupta 2016, Lazear and Oyer 2013). Finally, an important part of the monitoring process is the feedback received by the employee on a regular basis (Schleicher *et al.* 2018).

Sanctions: Formal incentives and punishments are key elements of the self-control system's control mechanisms. Regarding incentives, they may be the most controversial topic in control because many questions remain — even after a great deal of research, about their usefulness. We will delve into those arguments later.

Formal incentives include some form of pay, generally monetary, that is offered to motivate the performance of a job. Examples of formal incentives include monetary wages in the form of hourly rates or salary, bonuses, sales commissions, benefits packages, promotions, sales contests, and other forms of monetary compensation. Monetary pay is known to create extrinsic motivation, which is motivation from sources external to performing the job itself. Several of these examples can also be thought of as high-powered incentives (Williamson 1991), so-called because they generally motivate immediate and specific action (e.g., salary, wages, commissions). Other incentives, such as benefits packages, do not motivate such specific actions and can be referred to as low-powered incentives.

The argument for monetary incentives is clear. Research has found that production increases with increases in monetary incentives and decreases with decreases in monetary incentives (Jenkins *et al.* 1998). For this reason, they are described as the most potent of the formal rewards. Further, research has also found that increases in formal incentives convey symbolic meaning and status (i.e., the employee is doing particularly well and is held in high regard).

On the other hand, *crowding out* suggests that employees lose their intrinsic motivation for performance once they are paid (this is the reason that many blood banks tend not to pay for blood donations; Deci and Ryan 1985). That is, their intrinsic motivation to perform well and do a good job is crowded out by receiving substantive raises in monetary compensation. Another issue is that pay for performance forces employees to focus narrowly on rewarded tasks and avoid necessary but unrewarded tasks unless they are specifically paid to do so. Such employees are accused of being risk-averse and showing little imagination (Kohn 1988). In fact, Slater (1980, p. 39) says, "getting people to chase money ... produces nothing but people chasing money."

What does motivation theory say? In Jenkins *et al.*'s (1998) meta-analysis they cover the previously mentioned motivation theories and describe how they contribute to the money vs. performance debate.

- Expectancy theory suggests that employees will seek the extrinsic reward and perform at a high level of effort to attain the reward.
- Reinforcement theory believes that when money is tied to performance it reinforces performance.
- Goal-setting theory suggests that performance tied to monetary gain would allow employees to attain their goals, thus performing as specified.
- Cognitive evaluation theory indicates that financial incentives tied to performance will decrease intrinsic motivation, thus eroding performance.

The results of the meta-analysis supported the belief that monetary incentives will increase performance, thus supporting expectancy, reinforcement, and goal-setting theories. Monetary incentives work, although there may be a crowding-out factor to some extent. Thus, how can intrinsic motivation be maintained? Perhaps, low-powered incentives hold an answer. This may be why employers today supplement monetary payments with childcare services, gymnasiums, and other forms of non-monetary compensation.

Formal negative sanctions, or punishments, have not been studied in as near detail as formal positive sanctions. However, when objectives are not met, managers are often forced to apply, or threaten to apply, negative sanctions in the form of demotions, suspensions, undesirable work assignments, reprimands, and even dismissal (Luneneburg 2012). As expected, when an employee is punished there is often an increase in resistance to the organization in some form. Punishments tend to reduce morale, increase anxiety, resistance, and retaliation, although the way the punishment is applied may reduce the effect. Khan *et al.* (2020) found that procedural justice mediated the relationship between punishments and employee responsiveness, suggesting that the fairer the punishment procedure, the less negative the effect of the punishment on the employee.

The informal mode of self-control

Discussions of the informal mode of self-control are dominated by the consideration of *organizational culture*. O'Reilly and Chatman (1996, p. 157) describe organizational culture as "a *social control system* based on shared norms and values … that influence(s) members' focus of attention, shape interpretations of events, and guide attitudes and behavior (emphasis in the original)." That is, the culture of the organization is the informal and unwritten set of guidelines and norms that drives the organization's daily existence. Examples of organizational culture include informal agreements on dress codes, language used in meetings, beliefs and motivations of the employees, and the intention of how the organization is to treat its customers and other constituents. Organizational culture can be so powerful that it can enhance, or detract from, organizational performance. In fact, O'Reilly and Chatman (1996, p. 160) go so far as to make the point that it "may be a more powerful form of control in modern organizations than traditional formal controls."

Regarding the power of organizational culture, it can be described along two dimensions (O'Reilly 1989). The *intensity* dimension concerns the strength of the culture that is held by the organization's employees. As agreement in the beliefs, expectations, and norms of the organization increase, the intensity of the culture becomes more powerful. Also, the *consensus* dimension taps into the extent of agreement on cultural issues across different groups and individuals in the organization. As consensus increases, the power of the organizational

Table 4.1.   How Firm Policies Contribute to Corporate Culture

Positive Contribution to Firm Culture	Negative Contribution to Firm Culture
• Encouraging independent decision-making and risk-taking	• Squashing free speech via termination and demotion
• Fostering creativity	• Illegal monitoring of employee electronic communications
• Eliminating micromanagement	• Retaliation for forming unions
• Providing safe areas to express opinions	• Placing managers under undue pressure to terminate staff
• Replacing formal periodic evaluations with job dialogues	• Constant ratings by colleagues after meetings and at other times
• Allowing employees to set their own work tasks	• "Sunshining" misbehaviors in public
• Celebrating efforts, not just success	• Lack of adequate mentoring, education, and training
• Providing attractive amenities such as wellness centers, athletic facilities, recreation areas, and complimentary meals	• Exceedingly long work hours
• Working remotely	• Prioritizing the client over employees
• Providing internal and external education opportunities	• Encouraging employee tattling
• Seeking work-life balance	• Failing to follow workplace health and safety standards
• Setting clear expectations and encouraging employees to speak up	

culture increases. Many firms have strong reputations for having impactful and powerful organizational cultures. Many of these cultures are encouraged by management based on their incentives, sanctions, and other policies. It is quite clear that management can support a positive culture and contribute to a negative one. Such policies are listed in Table 4.1.

Two things are important to note. First, although we think of positive cultures and how effective they are, there are many firms where negative cultures exist. These may be filtered down from an authoritarian management style or from incentives that are seen by employees as controlling rather than motivational. Second, although culture is an informal construct, it can be affected by (that is, influenced by) a firm's formal establishment of guidelines, incentive packages, and other sanctions. Clearly, culture may affect employees both positively and negatively:

- Google is a consistent winner of best places to work awards, and it feels as if its support of corporate culture targeted at innovation, education, and fun is responsible. They provide both high- and low-powered incentives (such as high pay, gyms, sleep pods, and hair salons) to motivate employees to de-stress on the job or at home, if that is where they choose to work (Hakobyan *et al.* 2022).
- Netflix's core principle is "people over process." There is a great deal of trust in employees expressed by management, and it filters down into employees' freedom to make decisions without worrying about micromanagement from above. The employees focus on being creative and taking responsibility for their decisions. Employees feel it is safe to express their opinions and be more receptive to the opinions of others (Grove Human Resources.com 2022).
- Although Amazon's culture has improved in recent years, it hasn't always been a positive experience for many employees. At the time of this writing, Amazon is fighting its employees' attempts to form unions at several of its locations (Hsu and Selyukh 2022). More specifically, low performers at Amazon are annually culled in what might be considered a form of purposeful Darwinism. Not only does Amazon constantly turn staff over but there are also several rating systems in place that assess performance, tardiness, and the quality of comments in meetings and other performance activities. Amazon focuses on hiring a broad set of employees with highly varied backgrounds, but they must perform or they are quickly dismissed. This creates a competitive climate with excessive work demands including mandatory overtime (Garcia 2022).

These, and other examples of cultural control describe how the culture of an organization permeates virtually everything it does.

It is important to note the differences in the notion of organizational "group" and "firm". Individuals seek group identification (van Knippenberg 2000) in order to maintain their social identity as desired. Thus, employees seek groups of work colleagues or friends to share their norms, attitudes, and beliefs regarding their firm. A strong identification with the group suggests that employees may work for the group, not necessarily the firm. Still, if a strong cultural control is present (similar from group to group), such work can impact the performance of the firm positively. However, O'Reilly (1989) makes the point that not all cultural influence is for the good of the organization or firm. Things go awry and attitudes toward the organization can be quite negative, which have serious negative consequences for production and performance.

In fact, there has been a good deal of interest in whether, and to what extent, organizational culture is a positive or negative influence on firm outcomes. Although evidence is mixed (O'Reilly and Chatman 1996), it is suggested that the more the organization's norms and behaviors are aligned with its mission the more likely it is to provide an efficient contribution to performance outcomes.

Let us now examine the specific mechanisms of the informal mode of self-control, setting standards, monitoring, and sanctions. I think that we will find that the informal mechanisms are strongly driven by organizational culture. In fact, O'Reilly (1989) makes the distinct point that culture creates standards that guide the organization.

Setting Standards: The setting of standards refers to generally understood information that establishes the guidelines for operating an organization. Important to understanding informal guidelines is the *psychological contract*. The psychological contract is a mutual understanding, not a one-sided expectation, of the duties and responsibilities of the organization and the employee. It is a set of promises that commit one to future actions (Robinson and Rousseau 1994). Like a formal written contract, the parties expect its informal form to be binding.

The content of the psychological contract may be narrow and specific, or broad and general. Beliefs regarding future assignments, support from management, weekends worked, planned salaries or bonuses, and project deadlines may all be in the psychological contract. This allows efficient operations and suggests that neither party be held to the incomplete, often static formal contract. As conditions change or unexpected situations arise, the parties can maintain a functioning organization. That is, the psychological contract, unlike a formal contract, changes over the life of the relationship.

A key issue with the psychological contract is that it sets up an expected reciprocal relationship between the parties (Robinson and Rousseau 1994). The more one is expected to do for the other, the greater the expected reciprocity. In fact, this can be stated as an obligation to perform. Even though the psychological contract is an unwritten document, and the parties share the beliefs in the contract, there is no guarantee that the parties share a mutual understanding and interpretation of the terms.

Unfortunately, this may cause one party to interpret the other party's actions as violations to the contract. "A person promised market wages in exchange for hard work who does not receive them feels wronged. Broken promises produce anger and erode trust in the relationship and thus, are expected to have more significant repercussions than unmet expectations" (Robinson and Rousseau 1994, p. 247).

Similar to the notion of the psychological contract is *perceived organizational support* (POS; Rhoades and Eisenberger 2002). These expectations of support may include signals of bonding to the employee, such as higher wages, departmental budgets, and anticipated promotions. Although both the psychological contract and POS are symbolic of expected reciprocity, POS is a *one-sided* expectation of the commitment — in terms of specific details — that the organization has made to the employee. Two issues here are key. One, the POS includes the specific details of how the relationship is expected to work, giving the employee a road map for the standards that are established, albeit in an informal way. Two, because the POS, like the psychological contract, is based on expectations of reciprocity, the employee knows the role it should play in the present and the future, to execute its duties for the employer.

Employees gauge the fairness and acceptability of treatment as an indication of the value that the firm places on them. There are many other important dependent variables to the expectations created by POS (Rhoades and Eisenberger 2002), including employee commitment to the organization, affect toward the job, involvement (identification and interest) to the job, performance, desires to remain, and withdrawal behaviors.

We now consider the final topic in understanding how firms and employees learn the standards for engagement and performance of duties: *Idiosyncratic deals* (i-deals). I-deals are "customized features of employment that individual employees negotiate (to) supplement standardized work arrangements" (Liao *et al.* 2014). Not all employees have the same "deal" with their employers. Even though salaries and benefits might be the same, certain people may negotiate unique work hours, bonuses, early retirements, company cars, and more. In return, they are expected to share an additional burden of work responsibilities. These are quite common in academia in fact, where many highly productive professors have additional research funds, graduate assistance support, and travel budgets. I-deals are based on the differing needs — and desires — of employees. As needs change (the need for more money, more time off, etc.) special arrangements may be negotiated. From our perspective, we should know that the deals serve as revised guidelines to the traditional and usually codified standards of employment. As i-deals change, so does the employee's psychological contract regarding their work arrangement. Like other elements in this section on informal standards setting, i-deals are based on a norm of reciprocity.

There are four general types of i-deals (Liao *et al.* 2014):

- *Flexibility i-deals* allow employees to arrange their work schedules to more favorable circumstances. This form of i-deal is sometimes granted to employees who might become marginalized over time for their colleagues' perception of lower performance.
- *Developmental i-deals* allow the employee to advance its work skills to prepare for future and expected challenges. These may include attendance at special conferences, and they put the employee in a superior position when it comes to promotions and raises. Employees with developmental i-deals are often more highly committed and less likely to quit the organization.
- *Workload-reduction i-deals* result in less time on the job so employees can pursue personal goals such as childcare or leisure.
- Finally, *task i-deals* involve re-arranging the various aspects of the job itself. Employees with task i-deals report higher levels of job satisfaction.

In summary, the literature has provided a wide variety of how standards are set in an informal way. An obvious question remains: "What is the relationship between formal and informal standard setting?" For instance, one might wonder which of the two modes of standards is seen as the most important and attended to by the employees or management of the organization. Further, when formal and informal standards are in conflict, as is often the case with a firm with a strong or changing corporate culture, does one replace the other or are they both utilized depending on the situation. Surely, this would be confusing to the employees and management alike.

Monitoring: Informal monitoring arises for several reasons. First, direct supervision of employees may not be available. Second, information is often not available to those who monitor the breadth of services performed by employees. Third, the cost of gathering information may be prohibitive. Finally, the authority of the monitor may not be seen as legitimate. It is because of these cases and others that informal monitoring emerges gradually over time (O'Reilly 1989).

In informal monitoring cases, employees often engage in self-monitoring to ensure that they remain on track for rewards. The idea of self-monitoring is also found in the distribution channels literature as a way of making sure that a firm's goals remain in alignment with the partner (Gilliland *et al.* 2010). Employees are also observed by others in their social group to ensure that norms remain consistent and shared.

Sanctions: Informal sanctions include informal incentives and informal punishments provided by the organization, a group of employees within the organization, or the self. According to Black (1998), compensation is a form of social control. Thus, informal incentives may provide similar benefits as formal incentives, but possibly without the negative sentiments (feelings of being controlled, lack of intrinsic motivation, etc.). From the power perspective, informal incentives do not typically result in immediate increased financial compensation but are longer term and vaguer in nature.

Employees' affective feelings about the organization, identification, and job satisfaction all contribute to their motivation to continue to work positively for the organization. As these factors increase, so too do work productivity and other performance outcomes.

Typically, this form of incentive is only offered with little or no monetary compensation, so there is little chance of elbowing out intrinsic motivation for extrinsic motivation. Long-term incentives are conceived as a symbol of trust that pay-off will eventually come (Benabou and Tirole 2005). Second, there may be no financial aspect to this form of reward. Compensation in terms of respect and recognition from colleagues is important in maintaining intrinsic motivation.

Informal punishments are also prevalent to employees who break norms, social standards, fail at their job, or misbehave in other ways (see Zhong and Robinson 2021). Informal punishments include discouragement, avoidance, mistrust, and threats to turn in a perpetrator (Hollinger and Clark 1982). Such punishments are thought to deter negative behaviors, and the results may be severe and may include aggressive lying, ostracism, seeking revenge, guilt, shame, distrust, low self-esteem, and more (Zhong and Robinson 2021).

Discussion: Moving from the Self to the Other

This chapter has dealt almost exclusively with the control of the self in an organization. But what is the relationship between self-organizational control and interorganizational control? How do we get from the first to the next?

Several studies emphasize the importance of the individual in such a situation. Regarding trust, Zaheer *et al.* (1998) conceptualized trust as an individual-level concept, distinct but related to interorganizational trust, stating "it is *individuals* as members of organizations rather than the organizations themselves, who trust" (p. 141, emphasis in original), implying that individual actions affect organizational outcomes. Thus, trust is between boundary spanners. This origin of trust translates to organizational-level trust (also between boundary spanners of some type). Doney and Cannon (1997) examined buying firms' trust in their sales representative and found that the more the firm trusted the salesperson, the more positive traits they saw in the salesperson. Further, the more they trusted the supplier's salesperson the more positively they related to the supplier.

Additional papers by Heide and colleagues (Heide *et al.* 2022, Heide and Wathne 2006, Murry and Heide 1998) demonstrated the theoretic relationships between individuals and the roles they play in interorganizational exchange. Organizations can take on the persona of individual members, holding constructs like trust and even affect (emotional liking) as organizational, not personal. Murray and Heide (1998) discussed interpersonal attachments between boundary spanners of organizations to reduce goal misalignments through established selection and socialization. In their study of "friends and businesspeople" (Heide and Wathne 2006) the authors describe how organizations take on the roles of people to collectively set the logic of the firm. Reviewing several game theory studies, they describe how business partners take on the purely economic perspective of businesspeople in their choices, or friends who cooperate as a matter of principle. Finally, in a recent study, Heide *et al.* (2022) find that employees decide what they want to be as an organizational identity, and those roles are executed in dealing with other firms. They suggest that firms take on individual's roles and "create" three primary orientations in organizations. An *individualistic orientation* is one that looks out for itself, is logical and rational in decision-making, and is motivated to seek its own objectives. A *relational orientation* is one that focuses on the needs of itself and its partner and works for the good of both organizations. Finally, a *collectivist orientation* is concerned with a larger collective, or network. These are simple, but important examples of individuals' needs to control their own destiny and contribute to the control structure and culture of an organization.

Chapter 5

The Dyadic Control System

Dyadic governance has been a key area of study for many years as we seek to understand control phenomena. The primary contexts for this research have been the channels of distribution, supply chain, and buyer–seller relationship literature. Thus, we typically think of dyadic control as one party's attempts to control the actions, behaviors, and outcomes of another. This may take place within different organizations in a single firm, in a networked relationship, or in independent organizations that work with one another. As with the other control systems, the general model of control holds, there are two modes of control (formal and informal) and three general categories of control mechanisms (setting standards, monitoring, and sanctioning). We will investigate these in some detail.

The dyadic control system, our second of three control systems, concerns itself with both bureaucratic and relational exchange. Although research has typically studied bureaucratic and relational exchange as individual phenomena they are, obviously, present simultaneously (see Ouchi 1979). Granovetter (1985) explains that all economic transactions are wrapped in social conditions, thus it is not possible to have a purely economic or purely relational exchange. This is a key characteristic of social control theory. In fact, in a literature dominated by studies on formal means of control, Williamson (1975) speaks of an organization's "atmosphere" and Gibbons (2005) refers to an organization's "halo effect." Granovetter's notion of social embeddedness explains how the social side of the relationship often enhances the economic side via group norms, mentoring, loyalty, and innovation. Although there are downsides to close relationships as well, such as a threat of opportunism (Lado *et al.* 2008), it is generally assumed that the two modes of control, via their mechanisms, are present together (Cao and Lumineau 2015). Exceptions may be a truly transactional relationship, where norms, understandings, and expectations have not been nurtured, nor have they had time to develop. In fact, some would argue that relational control mechanisms are not even needed. Nonetheless, in most all cases they are.

Formal and Informal Dyadic Control

The existence of formal dyadic control can be found in just about any control theory (see Gilliland 2023 for a review). Organizational control discusses the formalized gathering of information through output and behavioral control (Ouchi 1979); transaction-cost economics (TCE) relies on a bureaucracy to manage transactions (Williamson 1991); contract theory is based on formal contracts (Antia and Frazier 2001, Mooi and Ghosh 2010); and governance theory bases control on unilateral control mechanisms (Antia *et al.* 2006, Heide *et al.* 2007). As discussed in Chapter 2, typically a written agreement or specific contract gives the controller the authority power to govern. It is through this authority power that control is manifest via its specific control mechanisms. It is the mechanisms, and the interfirm influence that emanates from them, that do the work in aligning controller and target goals. On the other hand, informal control mechanisms exist to accomplish the same thing. In fact, Jensen and Meckling (1976) suggest that organizations are just a set of formal and informal contracts. Together, formal and informal mechanisms act to keep a relationship on track.

However, many firms pay a price for ineffective or inappropriate application of formal control mechanisms. In fact, the control mechanism in itself is controversial. We will see a distinct pattern emerge as we examine the individual control mechanisms. For now, note that formal control mechanisms motivate specific backlashes against the controller. These are a function of firms that do not agree on goal sets and retaliate in some way. Such firms know where their bread is buttered and maintain the relationship, and certainly accept their incentive payments, thus, they tend to be in general compliance and do their job. But they respond in negative ways as well. So, it is common to find positive and, simultaneously, negative aspects to control. As control increases, we will find that compliance and performance also increase, but there may just as well be increases in retaliation and opportunistic behaviors. This pattern makes complete sense to Frey (1993), who suggests that firms will maximize their utility by either completely complying, leaving the relationship, or maintaining the relationship and behaving opportunistically to maximize revenue. Thus, some firms may cheat on expenses, misreport outcomes, and otherwise game the system.

The setting of standards

As identified in Table 5.1, standards for dyadic control relationships tend to be set through codified contracts. These contracts can be detailed or simple, formal or written on the back of a napkin. In fact, some argue that they can even be unwritten and based on mutual expectations. The idea of a contract is to level expectations, align goals, and force specific actions. Contracts can be referred to daily or stuck away in a file drawer and seldom referenced. Contracts vary in length of coverage but tend to be more efficient in short- and medium-term transactions (Gundlach and Murphy 1993), most likely because there tend to be fewer personal relationships and socially embedded situations in short contracts. Also, in a short contract, required changes and external disruptions are less likely. Contract efficiency is important because it maximizes the value of a

Table 5.1.   Dyadic Control System

Dyadic Control System	
Controller/Target of Control	*Controller.* One of the actors in the business partnership *Target.* The partner firm
Formal Control Mode Logical and rational thinking, calculative assessment, instrumental reasoning	Transactions of a short- or medium-term horizon. Bureaucratic, unilateral control driven by the authority of carefully specified contracts and power advantages *Setting Standards*: Simple and complex contracts and agreements *Monitoring*: Outcome and process monitoring *Sanctioning*: High-powered incentives, compensatory sanctions
Informal Control Mode Norms of understanding and behavior, affect, relational assessment	Personal and relational bonds between two parties, daily interaction is a function of two-way communication, agreed-upon modifications to plans, and mutually understood strategies and tactics. The written contract is seldom used in lieu of relational norms and general understandings *Setting Standards*: Informal or bilateral understandings *Monitoring*: Goal monitoring, self-monitoring *Sanctioning*: Low-powered incentives, therapeutic, and conciliatory sanctions

relationship (Carson and Ghosh 2019). Contracts are a glue that establishes and maintains relationships to a common understanding among participants, and they are a key factor in moving relationships forward.

Importantly, contracts are not complete. That is, there is no such thing as a perfect contract. The cost of writing a contract is high, as is enforcement of the contract, and not all potentially important elements can be considered (Wuyts and Geyskens 2005). Consider the COVID-19 disruption to business and consumer relationships. Countless contracts had to be modified, canceled, or ignored because global pandemics are seldom considered in contracts. Also, as markets change, new technologies are introduced, and new competitors enter, contracts may not adjust accordingly. Further, knowledge is imperfect, and not all issues are known at the time of codification.

Contracts are a license to control. They are supported in courts and can be legally enforced. Contracts contribute to a firm's authority power and give it the ability to govern a partner or network of partners. Although contracts may be debated and appealed, they can eventually result in punishments in terms of jail time, fines, adjustments to the structure of organizations, and more. Probably most damaging to a firm is the future losses that may accrue because of a court's decision.

There are primary dimensions to contracts, which can be described as soft (from the informal mode of control) and hard, or codified (Lusch and Brown 1996). A second dimension of a contract is its contents, that is, what is actually covered — or not — in the contract. The third, and probably most important dimension is the specificity of detail in the contract.

Specificity of the Contract. Contract specificity deals with how much of a potential transaction is covered in terms of clear definitions and controlling contract clauses. The more that is addressed in the contract, and the more that is clearly addressed, the greater the specificity. Generally, the more specific the contract, the less wrangling, which suppresses contract violations overall (Griffith and Zhou 2015). Further, as specificity increases there is less need to monitor the other party. The firm knows that they will be protected in court, should it come to that, if the contract is specific about the topic of concern. Thus, as specificity increases, the need to monitor the partner decreases (Kashyap *et al.* 2012).

Specificity is also a function of the culture of the relationship between the two parties (Wuyts and Geyskens 2005). The study of contracts and culture is especially important to consider for firms that are exporting across country boundaries. Of course, legal structures can be vastly different in foreign countries, but culture is also important. Generally, a positive culture between the contracting parties leads to less specificity because social norms plug contract gaps, so details are needed less, and norms are relied upon more. Also, different facets of contracts produce different amounts of specificity. When the partnership is characterized by uncertainty avoidance a more specific contract results. This is because those that have apprehension about the future need formal controls to guide them through the uncertainty. Specificity is also a characteristic of high-power distance cultures (differences in power structures between the upper and lower-class members of a society) because the less-powered party needs the details provided in a specific contract to protect its interests (Wuyts and Geyskens 2005).

What's in a Contract? Contracts cover a variety of topics, including purchasing agreements, licensing arrangements, and other vendor-related transactions, changes in switching costs, and, importantly, boundary-spanner situations such as franchising, distribution channels, and sales representatives (Gundlach and Murphy 1993). In contracts, pricing may be set, quantities and delivery dates established, location and building contracts agreed upon, and a host of other issues specified. Regarding how content affects outcomes, Mooi and Gilliland (2013) find two major elements in contracts based on the protection of the transaction. Studying clauses that protect the transaction covered, they found there to be more enforcement actions taken against the violators, but clauses that protect the relationship itself were found to have fewer enforcement actions. This is because relationship issues could be informally resolved because interaction guidelines were in place.

Contract Enforcement: The enforcement of contracts is one of the six key governance mechanisms to keep relationships on track as identified by Heide (1994). Contract enforcement includes discussing problems, formal punishments such as withholding of benefits, fines (say, for territory violations where violators often have to pay penalties to the firm violated), firings, and occasionally, legal action (Antia *et al.* 2006). Enforcement is often used to reduce dysfunctional behaviors such as grey marketing, dumping, non-compliance, and below-standard performance (Wang *et al.* 2013). Although enforcement is decreased in the presence of relational norms, it increases with transaction-specific assets, and the asymmetry and magnitude of interdependence (Antia and Frazier 2001).

Contractual Outcomes: The outcomes of contracts are in some cases surprising, although we shouldn't be surprised according to some researchers. Just like a prenuptial marriage agreement, Samaha *et al.* (2011) suggest that a contract inherently signals distrust. Actors often react to being put on notice with negative behaviors. For instance, Wuyts and Geyskens (2005) find that the more specific the contract, the more there is an opportunistic reaction. This finding is similar to Brown *et al.*'s (2006) finding that contract specificity drives conflict and, further, the more there is conflict in a relationship, the less fair the interactions seem. However, actual punishments reduce opportunism in the relationship (Antia *et al.* 2006) and Wang *et al.* (2013) find very positive results for punishment. It seems to decrease opportunism and, if the punishment is deemed to be fair it may even build trust in the relationship.

Soft Contracts: Soft, or psychological contracts (that is, unwritten) present themselves in dyadic relationships for several reasons. First, there are constraints on what contract law can efficiently cover. For instance, contracts tend to be less effective in the long term (Gundlach and Murphy 1993). Second, soft contracts may arise because of the costs associated with writing and drafting full contracts. Third, hard contracts signal distrust, so a soft understanding may emerge as an alternative way of working together. Fourth, soft contracts tend to emerge when firms are bilaterally dependent on one another (Lusch and Brown 1996). Finally, because informal relationships are embedded in formal relationships, soft contracts arise to fill in the many "holes" of a hard contract that exist because of the writing costs. Thus, soft contracts may stand alone or be used in conjunction with hard contracts. Regarding the culture that exists in the dyad, soft contracts are motivated by collective cultural affiliation because they are keen to focus on aligned goals (Wuyts and Geyskens 2005). Soft contracts are found to increase performance outcomes and motivate long-term relational behaviors (Lusch and Brown 1996). Also, from an enforcement perspective, firms are interested in confirming and motivating reciprocity and shared expectations. Finally, Brown *et al.* (2006) explain how the more a relationship is governed by explicit contracts, the more it leads to decreased satisfaction with the relationship by the target of control.

Monitoring

Monitoring partners has to do with surveillance of a partner's outcomes and/or behaviors to ensure that they are performing as is stated in their contract or agreement.[1] Many tasks can be monitored and reflect the established contract or distribution agreement. Standard monitoring characteristics for buyer–seller relationships

---

[1] Confusion exists over just what is monitoring, and how it differs from control. Some researchers have taken the notion of outcome and behavioral monitoring and built full governance schemes out of all activities that monitor *or attempt to influence* the trading partner. Thus, the terms "behavioral control" and "outcome control" may be confused with behavioral and outcome monitoring. We find that many researchers include the monitoring of outcomes and behaviors as part of their composite control construct. For parsimony, we attempt to distinguish studies of overall control from pure monitoring studies.

may include quality of the product, damages upon delivery, time of delivery, fit and function, R&D support, profit of the supplier/buyer, logistic variables, and more. Monitoring of distribution channel partners may include many from the previous list as well as marketing outcomes such as share, sales, margin, profitability, market penetration, and other easily measured outcomes, as well as more difficult-to-measure outcomes such as customer satisfaction. Also, floor plan participation, number of selling representatives, selling processes, and color, quality, and safety of franchise restaurants are all monitored. Minute and seemingly unimportant issues are commonly monitored as well: some hotel franchisors monitor the cotton count of towels and sheets, food franchisors monitor the colors of the service counters, and beer brewers monitor the temperature of beer distributors' cold storage facilities. The many topics and examples of monitoring are often classified into two categories, outcome (or output) monitoring and behavioral (or process) monitoring.

Not only is it important to monitor to ensure appropriate activities and outcomes in the field, Jensen and Meckling (1976) state that it is necessary to monitor whenever there is separation of ownership and management. This separation means that goals may be rarely shared, thus monitoring of some form is a necessity (Mukherji *et al.* 2007). Firms have disparate goals such as differences in product positioning, acceptable price points, product quality desired, and most other production and marketing variables.

Monitoring is related to our first control mechanism, setting standards, in that the standards direct firms as to what to monitor. Thus, monitoring is typically assessed via predetermined information (Grewal *et al.* 2013).

Monitoring has been a focus of the organizational control and agency literature since 1975 when Ouchi and Maguire studied how retail salesclerks' selling behaviors were monitored. Today, most all theories of control include the notion of monitoring or oversight of some kind to help ensure goal alignment. Still, in practice goals are often not aligned, monitoring may not be efficient, and conflict over expected actions occurs. In general, however, monitoring has been shown to work.

A key issue regarding monitoring is that it is one of the few theories where both formal and informal controls (the clan) are accommodated within the same structure (Jaworski 1988, Ouchi 1979). Generally, there are three categories of monitoring. These categories have been found to exist in the same relationship and are typically correlated with one another (see Eisenhardt 1985, Grewal *et al.* 2013), suggesting that there are high and low monitoring firms.

Eisenhardt (1985) suggests that the two general forms of control — outcome and behavior — are available as correction mechanisms based on the information that each provides. This allows the coexistence of firms with diverse goals. The information provided concerns the ability to count (outcome monitoring) or accurately observe (behavioral monitoring). The third form of monitoring (clan, informal, or bilateral monitoring) is a function of shared goals. So, when do we use each of the three monitoring forms?

Eisenhardt (1985, 1989) and Ouchi (1979) explain that monitoring is linked to available information. If tasks are easily programmable (say, a manager can easily outline the transformation activities of the sales process), behavioral monitoring is optimal. If not, and if outcome measures of success are available, outcome monitoring is best. If both knowledge of the transformation process and outcome measures are available, both are used (thus, the positive correlations between output and process found by Grewal and colleagues (Grewal *et al.* 2013)). Importantly, the monitoring of the activities or results allows management the necessary information to provide coordinating advice and influence to the agent. What happens when neither task programmability nor outcome measurability are available? At this point, the monitoring of the similarity and complementarity of attitudes and goals is applied. This is known as clan control, which we classify as an informal control mechanism. The notion of outcome, behavioral and clan monitoring, has been advanced by many governance and control theories.

Frey (1993) discusses some of the negative aspects of monitoring, such as reduced work effort, in terms of crowding out. Targets of control show less appreciation for the relationship with the controller because monitoring is a sign of distrust, which crowds out the positive effects of the relationship. Targets then act opportunistically to maximize the value of their relationship.

One thing to note, successful monitoring is unavailable to firms without a license to control. Without some form of authority, the outcomes may be counted and the behaviors documented, but the license to make changes due to this information is not available.

Outcome Monitoring: The point of outcome monitoring is to check for goal alignment as designed and dictated in setting standards. There are many reasons that firms monitor outcomes, the most obvious being they have access to outcome information. This is generally attainable through end-of-month reporting, sales reports, and other financial data. As mentioned above, although this data might not always be trustworthy, it is often the only data available, particularly if behavioral information is difficult to attain or prohibitively expensive. Relatedly, firms outcome monitor when the transformation process or task programmability is not known. The classic example is in international export environments where psychic distance is high and little is known or understood about the selling process. Kashyap *et al.* (2012) find that when extracontractual incentives are at stake outcome monitoring (as well as behavioral monitoring) is more prevalent to protect the availability of the incentives. However, Celly and Frazier (1996) demonstrated that environmental uncertainty actually reduces the use of outcome monitoring. This is because an uncertain environment increases the error gap between verifiable performance and total outcomes, and many targets realize that more activities are out of their control when uncertainty is high.

Regarding the effects of outcome monitoring, they are quite positive. One of the jobs of outcome monitoring is to reduce opportunism, and this has been found to occur in some cases. For instance, Kashyap *et al.* (2012) find that outcome monitoring motivates compliance and reduces opportunism. Heide *et al.* (2007) also found that outcome monitoring reduces opportunism. Outcome monitoring also has positive effects on performance goals (Bello and Gilliland 1997). However, Grewal *et al.* (2013) found an interesting inverted-U shape when plotting the effects of outcome performance, suggesting that peak performance occurs at medium levels of outcome monitoring. Finally, Crosno and Brown's meta-analysis (2015) generally found positive aspects of outcome control.

Behavioral Monitoring: The results of behavioral monitoring are not quite as positive. Behavioral monitoring, and the influences that follow, encroach on the target's standard way of doing business. The monitoring process implies that the target doesn't "know what it is doing" and insists on changing the behaviors of the target. As the target pushes back against such pressure it is less likely to achieve goals (in the eyes of the controller). This is particularly troubling when the controller has inadequate information regarding the transformation process, and it is unable to accurately specify — let alone assess — the programmability of the task. International exporting or selling in new or unfamiliar markets are prime examples of the problem. Nonetheless, as the perception of task programmability increases, the use of the behavioral monitoring mechanism increases (Eisenhardt 1985).

The often-negative outcomes of behavioral monitoring are problematic as well. Kashyap *et al.* (2012) found that behavioral monitoring actually increased opportunism and at the same time decreased compliance. The second result is understandable, the first not so much. We can speculate that in order to not waste their time and effort, and thus their costs, the target of control might obfuscate their transaction process to the controller. This opportunistic finding is reflected in Heide *et al.* (2007) and confirmed in Crosno and Brown's (2015) control meta-analysis. Thus, it seems that divergent goals cannot be aligned quite as easily as we would hope.

Clan Monitoring: Fortunately, there is an "on the other hand" and that has to do with what happens when goals are aligned. The social side of dyadic exchange may provide an opportunity for parties from different organizations to share goals, which has several effects on the monitoring process (see Gilliland *et al.* 2010). When goals are shared or when there is a base level of trust between the parties, outcomes have been shown to improve in terms of resource accumulation, volume of services offered, operating efficiency, and flexibility (Bouillon *et al.* 2006). Also, when goals are shared there is simply less need to monitor. It would be hard for trust and relational norms to develop without sharing goals. Surveillance of behaviors and outputs decreases as firms contribute to the betterment of the dyad. However, two forms of monitoring arise. Because shared goals allow the relationship to progress, firms monitor the goal directions of their partner (see Gilliland *et al.* 2010, Ring and Van de Ven 1994) to ensure that a long-term horizon, and all the investments necessary to support that, are still safe. Further, the controller self-monitors, to make sure that it is maintaining alignment with its target. In summary, in a clan environment, firms still monitor, yet in quite different ways.

Sanctioning

The third mechanism of dyadic control involves sanctioning. Sanctioning is the positive or negative payoff based on monitoring information. Sanctions can also be referred to as "rewards" or "punishments." Monitoring, formal or informal, usually provides the information for sanctions to be fairly distributed, although that clearly is not always the case.

Formal Incentives and the Incentives Myth: Paying compensation is one of the key elements of control (Crosno and Brown 2015). Incentives are an important control mechanism as they are designed to align the target's goals to those of the controller, and motivate target performance (Benabou and Tirole 2003). Incentives serve as a signal that positive intentions for a future relationship exist, which reduces the partner's uncertainty about future engagement (Scott and Connelly 2011).

Incentives paid by the controller to the target are perhaps the most powerful of the three control mechanisms in terms of motivating shared goals. Because contracts are incomplete, the incentive offers payment (say, commission, margins, discounts, license fees, bonuses, rebates, or royalties) for the performance of a broad set of activities all designed to bring the target's behavior in line with those as desired by the controller (Holmstrom and Milgrom 1994). Williamson (1991) describes how incentives, particularly monetary incentives, are powerful motivators to perform in the immediate term. Targets of control are motivated by more than money, as we shall discuss, but money is the main reason for performance. The amount of money paid as an incentive, and the nearness of it being paid to actual performance, the higher the utility of the target. This is key because, if the target's utility for staying in the relationship drops below its utility for leaving the relationship it will exit, perform alternative tasks, or game the system in some way to make up for its losses (Gibbons 2005). Unlike non-monetary incentives (such as marketing support), or incentives whose payment is delayed (such as reimbursement for floorplan investments), high-powered incentives are preferred by targets. Immediate monetary payments make up for inefficiencies in low-powered incentive payments in two ways (Gibbons 2005). First, events beyond the target's control occur: economies deteriorate, uncertainties and volatility increase, and competition strengthens. All of these and more may increase the difficulty of selling or performing for the partner.

Further, there is noise in the measurement system, suggesting that a target's outputs are uncertain. Such occurrences reduce returns for targets and cause them to seek other sources of income (Oyer 1998).

An incentive, a form of compensation designed to compensate a target for performing as directed, is actually a portfolio of instruments. In my investigation of information technology distributors (Gilliland 2003), I found five general types of support provided to resellers, which tend to run the gamut between high- and low-powered. These included:

- *Monetary Incentives*: Used to control reseller outcomes, include bonuses, margins, discretionary income, and financial programs.
- *Marketing Development Support*: Used to control the reseller performance of channel functions, include market development tools, personal assistance, and certification programs.
- *Supplemental Contact*: Above and beyond the ordinary contact to control quality content of channel functions, include automated information and transactions.
- *Credible Channel Policies*: To control reseller participation, include pledges of investments and conflict resolution strategies.
- *End-User Encouragements*: To control the benefits of long-term relationships, include reseller marketing programs and co-marketing.

But do incentives work? Theoretically, yes, and they are seen as a great motivator for performance and an explanation for reducing the risk that agents must absorb. However, there is an alternative view of incentives, which I refer to as the "incentive myth." Many researchers have found, like other formally applied control mechanisms, that using incentives to align goals may be problematic.

In fact, incentives often do not work for several reasons. First, monetary incentives are weak enforcers over time. At best, "monetary incentives (are) a blunt instrument" (Akerlof and Kranton 2005, p. 11) because they are based on observable output or behavior only. However, because all tasks are not visible (Fehr and Gachter 2000), the performance of all tasks cannot be rewarded. Logically, there is an overemphasis on behaviors that are recognizable (Gibbons 2005) compared to those that are not. Thus, profit may be endangered over time because true output is difficult to measure, quality performance is often undetectable (Lazear 2000), and eventually, the magnitude and focus of effort induced by incentives are often unsatisfactory (Acemoglu *et al.* 2007). Second, monetary incentives can be demotivational. Bouillon *et al.* (2006, p. 270) state, "heavy reliance on financial incentives could undermine performance and ... willingness to cooperate." Although incentives are designed to motivate specific behaviors, they can demotivate agents because they are seen as controlling (Ryan and Deci 2000), leading to gaming of the system (Gibbons 2005). When interpreted as such, the controlled party often displays a lack of effort, a failure to comply, and reduced intrinsic motivation (Deci *et al.* 1999). The intensity of effort is also reduced because of noise in the performance measure (Feltham and Xie 1994); agents will not put forth adequate effort if there is uncertainty in the payoff. Third, operant conditioning suggests purchasers become trained to seek deals while postponing typical purchasing behaviors. To the purchaser, as rewards are recognized via the offered discount (response to the reward in operant terms), additional deals offered (reinforcement) solidify the relationship between satisfaction and reception of the incentives (Blattberg and Neslin 1990). Thus, there are several possible negative impacts on the firm offering the incentive. Because conditioning "trains" customers to look for deals, they pack their inventory with discount-offered goods, causing principal margins to suffer. Finally, Kerr (1975) notes "the folly of rewarding A while hoping for B"; that is, the folly of incenting one or a few tasks (i.e., only paying sales margins) while hoping that a constellation of activities is appropriately achieved. However, margins pay only for outcomes, ignoring non-incentivized but still important tasks. In a channels setting for instance, the principal may feel that generous margins pay the agent to perform adequate market development, applications assistance, and after-sales service, but the agent is more interested in skimping on cost-inducing non-incented tasks and focusing on margin-producing tasks alone (Benabou and Tirole 2003). Thus, the incentive itself can lead to dysfunctional activities by rewarding the wrong behavior (Baker 2002).

A final issue is crowding out. One area of interesting research has been on the substitution or complementation of formal and informal control. When both are present in a dyadic relationship, do they complement one another — that is, do social norms fill the gaps in the formal incomplete contract — or does one control mechanism replace the other? Fehr and Gachter (2000) investigated the substitution of formal controls for informal when both were present. They proposed that a norm of reciprocity holds all relationships together and that formal incentives (and punishments) damage that norm. Thus, formal incentives contribute to the potential destruction of relationships. Lazzarini *et al.* (2004) explained a similar effect by suggesting that formal controls violated any social norms on which the relationship existed. Much more is to be done in this area.

I could go on. Fortunately, informal incentives provide us with a clearer path to progress.

Informal Incentives: We may refer to informal incentives as bilateral incentives (Gilliland *et al.* 2010) or low-powered incentives (Obadia *et al.* 2015). Either way, informal incentives are motivations to perform based on shared goals. When goals are shared there is less reason to force alignment between parties because the firms, if not already aligned, intend to be.

Such situations can best be explained by stewardship theory, a spin-off of agency theory. Stewardship (Wasserman 2006) assumes goals are aligned between parties and the relationship is based more on identification with the other party. Thus, when goals are aligned, efficiencies arise and utilities increase. Risk is shared between the controller and the target as long as goals remain aligned, which decreases the negative exposures to uncontrollable circumstances. In this under-researched theory, it is questionable what might happen if goals went out of alignment. Some might say that as long as there is identification and trust the relationship would maintain. Others might argue that if goals are misaligned, utilities are no longer maximized, and the relationship would suffer (like any other agency relationship).

Relying on agency theory and stewardship theory, Gilliland and Kim (2014) tested whether the effects of the extent of agreement with a partner's incentive goals resulted in positive outcomes. They found two dimensions of incentive agreement, instrumental evaluation (the extent the incentive had sufficient magnitude and reduced the overall costs of operations) and congruence evaluation (the extent that the incentive portfolio was a fit with its own strategic direction). As instrumental evaluation increased, compliance was achieved, but the resellers shirked more. On the other hand, as congruence evaluation increased compliance was reduced, as was shirking. The findings hold with Dyer and Singh's (1998) notion that when goals are aligned, the transparency and reciprocity in the relationship discourage free riding. They also suggest that when knowledge sharing, trust, and goodwill abound, it is the least costly form of control and utilities are naturally maximized.

Regarding low-powered incentives, Williamson (1991) describes these incentives that do not provide immediate or even certain payoffs. In Obadia *et al.*'s (2015) exporting study they operationalized incentives as conflict resolution strategies, territory protection, market development support, training, and managerial advice. They found positive relationships between low-powered incentives and relationship quality and transaction-specific investments. No such relationships were found between high-powered incentives and the same dependent variables.

Punishments

Much less is known about punishments at the dyadic level than is known about incentives. Punishments come in both formal and informal measures. Formal punishments generally occur when an agent or dealer somehow violates an explicit contract. Examples include territory violations, pricing outside of agreed-upon prices and margins, violations of operational requirements, stealing potential customers from other dealers, and more. Other violations may be of the informal kind, i.e., the breaking of soft or psychological contracts. These may include violations of gentleman's agreements regarding territory definitions, carrying competing lines, and informal pricing/margin understandings. Sanctions as punishments also come in formal (fines, margin reductions, compensations paid for future losses, cancellation of discounts) and informal (lack of attention paid, and adjusting the order of new product distribution) ways.

Shared Goals and Trust

Shared goals

Even though our topic is control, we cannot deny the importance of goals, short-term or long-term, shared or discrepant. In fact, all informal control mechanisms used seem to hinge on shared goals. Here's what we know:

- Informal contracts focus on aligned goals (Wuyts and Geyskens 2005). In fact, if goals are not aligned, informal control may not be available.
- Informal contracts increase performance outcomes (Lusch and Brown 1996). Relationships become more efficient and less costly as contractual disputes decrease.

- Informal control is a function of shared perspectives and goals (Ouchi 1979). Thus, social-based contracts are available.
- When goals are shared there is less reason to force alignment (Obadia *et al.* 2015). Firms tend to fall into place automatically.
- When goals are shared, efficiencies increase (Wasserman 2006), as does utility. Thus, shared goals make it more likely that exit is not required and the relationship will endure.
- If goals are not shared, short-term control in the form of monitoring increases (Mukherji *et al.* 2007). Unfortunately, monitoring is a sign of distrust.

There is no doubt that shared goals are important. They are the entryway way for informal controls and trust to emerge. But, is that always a good thing?

Trust ... and formal control

A key issue in IOR relationships regards one firm's propensity to trust another and the determinants of this inclination to trust. Previous research has found that various situations result in trusting behaviors such as shared goals and norms (Zucker 1986), control circumstances (Vosselman and van der Meer-Kooistra 2009), good-will, and various risk-reduction techniques (Das and Teng 2001). These perspectives tend to view trust as a positive component of a healthy relationship, resulting in satisfactory outcomes and long-term exchange (Bijlsma-Frankema and Costa 2005). In fact, from a practitioner's perspective, Donald Fites, previous CEO of Caterpillar, Inc. said, "The quality of the relationship ... is much more important than the contractual agreements or techniques and tactics ... what matters is trust" (Fites 1996, p. 85). Powerful words.

On the other hand, others have suggested a dark side to trust, with trust being responsible for motivating corruption, lowering levels of vigilance as well as safeguarding and cheating behaviors (Das and Teng 2001, Gargiulo and Ertug 2006).

However, like trust, formal control is complex. So, what happens when trust and formal control are considered simultaneously? Previous work has suggested a variety of sometimes-discrepant findings, including that formal control and trust are positively intertwined (Vosselman and van der Meer-Kooistra 2009); formal control, in terms of monitoring, can destroy trust (Bijlsma-Frankema and Costa 2005); trust reduces the costs of negotiation, allowing less formal types of control to substitute for more formal types (Zaheer *et al.* 1998), contractual governance is positively related to trust (Cao and Lumineau 2015); and formal control and trust substitute for one another (Dekker 2004).

Trust has been found to be a key proponent in the building of long-term relationships (Doney and Cannon 1997). Trust acts as a quasi-governance mechanism (Bijlsma-Frankema and Costa 2005; cf. Braddach and Eccles 1989) and typically reduces opportunism brought about by uncertainties in relationships (Pfeffer and Salancik 1978), allowing firms to work harder for one another (Anderson *et al.* 1987). Trust begins at the contract level — "thin" or contract-based trust — and becomes more "thick" as it expands to uncodified issues in the relationship (Barney and Hansen 1994; Vosselman and van der Meer-Kooistra 2009). Trust lubricates the relationship by promoting volunteer behaviors among the parties (Bachmann 2001, Bijlsma-Frankema and Costa 2005). Such extra-role behaviors are possible because trust can occur at the interpersonal as well as the institutional level (Bachmann 2001, Doney and Cannon 1997). Trust reduces the cost of governance as it avoids contracting costs, facilitates contract adaptation, and requires less monitoring (Lado *et al.* 2008). It also reduces opportunism and increases communication in the dyad (Fang *et al.* 2008).

At the same time, trust is a willingness to accept vulnerability (Schoorman *et al.* 2007), and when a firm trusts it naturally drops its guard and reduces monitoring behaviors, making it vulnerable to firms with hidden agendas (Das and Teng 2001). Other dark side circumstances exist with trust (Lumineau 2017). For example, firms begin to lack objectivity, encouraging strategic blindness and reducing constructive discourse. Because trust exposes the more trusting party to cheating and opportunism (Lumineau 2017), it increases the riskiness of the relationship and often puts the trusting firm in a precarious position. It also takes an inordinate amount of time and money to establish (Bachmann 2001). However, Gundlach and Cannon (2010) suggest an alternative view to this dark perspective on trust. First, they note the high failure rate of many trusting firms, and suggest it is due to poor results in the trust-performance linkage. They find that verification of activities between firms (in their words, "trust but verify") shores up this linkage. Such verification activities include monitoring (as we might expect), information exchange, and formal firm reviews.

What happens at the nexus of control and trust is under debate. There are three perspectives to consider. The first perspective is that control and trust are causally linked, although the direction of this linkage is not clear (Emsley and Kidon 2007). Tomkins (2001) and Vosselman and van der Meer-Kooistra (2009) find that trust starts with formal control. When formal mechanisms are in place, it provides a safe platform for trust, which may grow with time. On the other hand, Bijlsma-Frankema and Costa (2005) note that trust reduces the need for formal control processes. The second perspective is that trust and control are substitutable; either trust or control, but not both, safeguard the relationship. Others (Dekker 2004, van der Meer-Kooistra and Vosselman 2000) disagree. Their perspective suggests that trust and control are complementary, they work together to stave off opportunism and guide the relationship (Dekker 2004). Interestingly, Gulati and Nickerson (2008) found evidence of both substitution and complementation effects of trust and control. We will address these issues more thoroughly in the latter chapters.

Discussion: More on Goal Alignment

Let's revisit goal alignment from a broader perspective in Figure 5.1. As discussed, goal alignment comes in two forms: short-term alignment and long-term alignment. In the short term, control mechanisms are aimed at specific transactions and protecting those transactions for a limited period. Thus, they tend to be formal, because formal controls are not long-term oriented, they are more interested in control in the here and now. Thus, contracts arise, monitoring is implemented, and the relationship moves forward, or not, depending on satisfactory sanctions. If sanctions are positive and the relationship is on track, positive outcomes of control are the result. These include highly efficient production and output (the goals are aligned), the meeting of standards of performance, and compliance by the target to the total governance scheme.

What happens if the contract is unreasonable or short-sighted, monitoring is mishandled, and sanctions are onerous? While

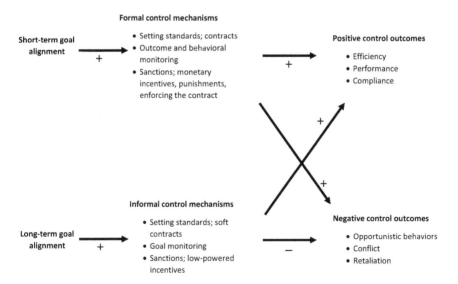

Figure 5.1. The Role of Goal Alignment in a Dyadic Setting

compliance may be forced, the relationship may be subject to negative outcomes such as opportunism from the weaker party, conflict, and even retribution. Thus, short-term goal alignment results in formal control circumstances, which will help and/or harm the relationship.

In a perfect world, effective short-term goals may align the relationship, allowing long-term goals to emerge as managers understand how they may work together and reap benefits from the performance of in-role and extra-role behaviors. This is possible and can be supported by more informal control mechanisms. The informal mechanisms allow firms to trust and take risks with one another. As informal controls smooth the relationship, efficiencies arise, performance is enhanced and opportunism, shirking, and other negative behaviors may be reduced. Thus, shared goals may be one of the most important characteristics of control.

Chapter 6

The Third-Party Control System

This chapter concludes our basic investigation into the systems, modes, and mechanisms of control. In Chapter 4, we examined control that emanates from the firm applied to itself (the controller and the target of control are one and the same). In Chapter 5, we examined control that emanates from the controller applied to the dyadic exchange partner. In this chapter, we will take a different perspective on control and discuss how the controller exists outside of the exchange dyad and exerts its control forces on one or both parties inside the dyad. In fact, in this discussion of third-party control the target is often a group of firms doing business with one another or a network of firms.

To provide key examples, we will look at control attempts as they emanate from industry trade associations and regulators, two powerful entities that keep a watchful eye over business transactions across most all industries. Both, particularly regulators, can be described as "quasi-governmental" controlling bodies.

Trade associations are typically large independent bodies that are sponsored by, and work for the interests of, members of a particular industry. In the US, there are over 22,000 trade associations, and there are an estimated additional 22,000 worldwide. Some of the more recognizable trade associations in the US are the American Bar

Association, the American Medical Association, the National Association of Home Builders, and the Independent Insurance Agents and Brokers of America. We recognize some of their promotional campaigns including the long-running "Got Milk" campaign by the California Milk Processing Board and "Beef. It's what's for Dinner" by the National Livestock and Beef Board. Worldwide, leading trade associations include the Australian Retailers Association, the European Steel Association, and Canada's Venture Capital and Private Equity Association.

Trade associations, funded by industry members, play a critical role in how an industry operates as they advance trade laws, foster networking among rivals, lobby regulators for favorable regulations, and offer resources such as industry best practices. They also work to regulate industry prices, create and impose ethics codes to enhance moral behaviors, provide legal counsel and advice on contracts, create information-sharing systems, do market research, establish accounting and safety standards, and advise on appropriate working hours and transportation techniques. One of their most important activities is lobbying while adhering to specific IRS laws and codes. In fact, it is said that trade associations often "shape the process of legislation" (Rajwani *et al.* 2015, p. 232). This may be particularly helpful if, as accused, government agencies are rude, abusive, unhelpful, and or otherwise unreasonable (Braithwaite *et al.* 1987, Job *et al.* 2007).

The power of the trade association should not be underemphasized. For example, the Pharmaceutical Research and Manufacturers of America (PhaRMA) "coordinated a $150 million advertising campaign ... to its members in support of the 2010 Affordable Care Act. More troublingly, an investigation launched by the Subcommittee on Oversight and Investigations confirmed that PhRMA was so influential that the Obama White House felt compelled to 'cut a deal' with PhRMA to promote and ultimately pass the controversial health care bill" (Rajwani *et al.* 2015, p. 225). In fact, many feel that trade associations go too far in influencing governmental policies.

In the United States, *regulatory agencies* are supported by national and state government mandates to enforce laws that regulate a broad set of arenas including advertising, trade rules, consumer protection, communications, workplace safety, food safety, antitrust, protection of the environment, and so forth. The legislature determines the limitations and breadth of an agency's responsibilities. Regulators monitor and investigate firms and organizations to abide by their requirements and they have the ability to fine and even shut down violators to ensure compliance. A key area of regulation is the financial industries, where the regulator detects and prevents fraud, keeps markets transparent, and ensures that the public is treated fairly. In the US, some of the most important regulators are the Federal Trade Commission, the Federal Communications Commission, the Securities and Exchange Commission, the Occupational Safety and Health Administration, the Consumer Product Safety Commission, and the Federal Election Commission.

Control Characteristics of Trade Associations and Regulatory Agencies

Generally, both trade associations and regulatory agencies use their licenses of control to guide behaviors and enforce policies on firms that they are responsible for monitoring. Although both licenses rely on the power of their position, their sources of power are quite different. While regulators govern at the behest of government legislation, trade associations earn a right to govern at the will of their members. The members sponsor the association and ask for many services from the association, the primary of which is lobbying the government and its regulatory representatives. This creates typically high levels of mutual dependence between the association and its members.

The third-party control process

Because regulatory agencies are supported by the legal system it gives them enormous latent power. Such power is used to motivate businesses to comply with legislation to make the world a better place. When compliance is not achieved, regulatory bodies move forward with negative sanctions such as fines, seizure of assets, and even incarceration (Lange 2008). However, it's a bit more complex than that, as is indicated in Figure 6.1.

Although some regulation arises from the legislative system, more often than not, regulation is organically derived from activities in trade and industry. This often occurs when firms feel that they are facing unfair or impractical competitive situations or that their hands are tied by existing regulation. For instance, in the building industries changing electrical and safety codes — to accommodate industry innovation — often mean unrecoverable costs to builders, electricians, and others. Firms, if powerful enough, can lobby the government

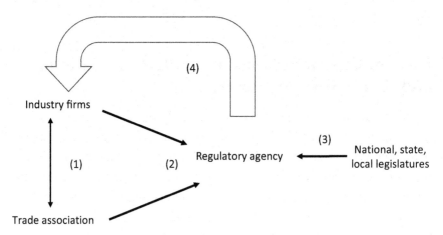

Figure 6.1.   Third-Party Control Process

Notes:
(1) Firms attempt to influence the trade association regarding their regulatory desires.
(2) Firms and trade association attempt to influence the regulatory agency.
(3) Legislative authorities pass laws, rules, and standards to be enforced by regulatory agencies.
(4) Regulatory agency imposes regulation on industry firms.

directly, but the far more usual path to have situations remedied is to work with their trade association. Trade associations, which exist for their members, gather others' opinions and may conduct original research to make a supporting case for the industry. Oftentimes issues are worked out within the industry through the establishment of guidelines and best practices, but sometimes not. If not, the trade association will use its power and expertise to convince its members to change behaviors or activities in a certain way. Thus, in these cases regulation often becomes unnecessary. If they can't be solved in such a way both firms and the trade association may lobby the appropriate regulatory body for support. Work has shown that older, larger, stronger-resourced firms are likely to join with trade associations in lobbying and communications efforts to support the trade association in their negotiations with the regulatory body (Cavazos 2007). If successful, the regulatory guidelines may change, as does the inspection, monitoring, and oversite process for the industry.

Thus, it is worth noting that familiar interorganizational power interactions take place. The regulatory agency may bend to the needs and influence of the trade associations and the firms it represents.

Why control is necessary

Regulatory control is often seen as a shackle to profit-seeking firms, although their attitudes toward regulation may be short-sighted. Safety rules, environmental protection legislation, and consumer protection regulations all cost money and potentially act as a drain on profits. Thus, many firms respond negatively to new or existing regulations. However, firms that resist regulation may do so for quite innocent reasons. Many firms are simply unaware of the complex rules and regulations, and they don't recognize that potential issues exist (May 2005, Sinclair 1997). Others may be unable to afford the costs of adhering to expensive new requirements. In fact, if a longer-term perspective was taken, firms might realize that regulation keeps them from harm by preventing expensive lawsuits and other forms of retaliation, such as boycotts, from constituents.

Other firms may not be so innocent. The franchising business has long been criticized for outright dishonesty in the application and onboarding processes of franchisors (Antia *et al.* 2013). The Federal Trade Commission requires franchisors' disclosure of information to potential franchisees. Typical complaints about franchisors surround misrepresentation of estimated earnings and franchise failures. Such complaints are so plentiful that many states have passed special legislation to prevent misrepresentation of this type. Further, some franchisors have been reprimanded and fined for using the "for good cause" phrase to illegally terminate less-than-successful franchisees.

Control perspectives

Formal Control: As with first- and second-party control, third-party control can be understood by considering the modes of control. Known as "regulatory culture," regulators use both formal and informal modes to control constituents. Formal legislation is seen as by-the-book control, with punishment by imprisonment as the ultimate sanction (May *et al.* 2005). In this mandatory compliance approach, the government plays a central role as it fines or punishes the accused violator. A key issue is that the regulator acts in a reactive way to violations, only acting as the legal stipulations are broken or ignored.

Formal control takes a *command-and-control* perspective. The regulator is in charge and controls the market by force. Command-and-control has an orientation toward prosecution of regulations instead of an avoidance of prosecution. One-size-fits-all in such an environment (Job *et al.* 2007) and there is little tolerance for evasion or delay. The targets of regulation may comply, but it tends to be out of fear (May 2005). However, when the command-and-control mode is in place, problems arise due to the agencies' constituents fighting back. Many firms fight back against the legislation by claiming some regulators are abusive, costly, and inefficient, all of which stifle innovation. Such conflict has caused stagnancy in regulation as there is sometimes a reluctance of the agency to prosecute and a reluctance of the courts to impose maximum punishments, resulting in a "barrage of criticism" from constituents (Sinclair 1997, p. 529).

Informal Control: As always, an alternative to formal control is the informal control mode. The point of informal control is to attain compliance without using the formal legal process (Braithwaite *et al.* 1987). The regulator, instead of playing the role of the police, uses other means to coordinate the relationship and gain compliance with its requirements. Known as "passive enforcement" (Grabosky 1995), the regulator persuades, cajoles, and otherwise tries to convince the firm of the value — and the requirements — of the regulation. This approach is also known as "regulation by raised eyebrows" (Braithwaite *et al.* 1987). Instead of being reactive, informal regulatory cultures are proactive as they move to educate, inform, and prevent violations. When informal control is used, the point is to motivate voluntary compliance on the part of the constituents (May 2005). The proactive approach gives the agency a chance to engage the firm before rules are violated. The agency seeks compliance by negotiation, consultation, diagnosis, or conciliation (Braithwaite *et al.* 1987). Interestingly, this approach creates a duty, or obligation for the firm to comply (May 2005).

Costs of third-party control

As discussed, agencies govern by the implementation of formal and informal mechanisms, as is the case in self- and dyadic-control situations. While this decision to use formal or informal control is the subject of a subsequent chapter, for now let's discuss how costs play a significant role in this choice.

First, Grabosky (1995) explains how there is no "magic bullet" solution as to which control apparatus to apply to any particular situation. Rather, a combination of policy tools may be designed and implemented, and this combination may be different for different situations. Thus, in many cases, formal and informal control mechanisms may overlap. The most salient reason for the designed assortment is the effectiveness of the tools. Depending on the target, its extent of agreement, the extent of violations, and the acceptance of the role of the regulator, the most effective combination is used. However, if a specific policy can be achieved via alternative methods, costs matter.

General costs include the writing and implementation of the rules, costs of inspection, monitoring, and prosecution. There are also potentially significant social costs in regulatory control. Grabosky says, "(t)he social impact of public policies can be profound; such impacts may extend directly or indirectly to individual or corporate motivation, to interpersonal relations, and to the fabric of trust in society. They can enhance or detract from the legitimacy of government, they may expand or curtail political freedom" (1995 p. 258). Such social costs are difficult to calculate, but possibly more important than the costs of managing the regulation. Perhaps costs can be weighed along with the importance of other factors such as personal liberty and consumer safety. It is clearly complex.

Agreement

A key element regarding control in this space is the extent to which the target agrees with the regulator's role and the regulations that are being advanced by the regulatory body (Gilliland and Manning 2002). Whether and how much the target agrees will influence the type of control mechanisms used. When the target agrees with the regulations, it understands the necessity and importance of the requirements. Control mechanisms in use are also a function of

Table 6.1. Characteristics of Agreement in Third-Party Control

	Agreement with Regulations	Disagreement with Regulations
Formal Control (Prosecution Orientation)	• Likely acceptance of regulations • Command and control • Deterrence: Threats of fines and imprisonment	• Likely rejection of regulations • Demand for by-the-book conformance • Threats, and follow-through, with fines and imprisonment
Informal Control (Persuasion Orientation)	• Voluntary acceptance of regulations • Regulatory reasonableness • Threats, fines not needed • Passive enforcement • Education, and tax and revenue inducements persuade conformance	• Likely rejection of regulations • Persuasion and cajoling, • Negotiation, education, loans, grants, tax credits to decrease the probability of rejection

the control mode (formal or informal). As Table 6.1 demonstrates, control can change based on the regulator's task at hand.

When the target of control believes that the proposed regulations are fair and necessary, it is likely to respond by accepting the regulation and conforming as required. But what is fair and necessary? Legal scholars suggest that agreement can be based on three motives of the firm that is the target of control (Nielsen and Parker 2012). These motives to agree and comply are the following: an *economic motive*, whereby compliance will maximize the firm's economic utility. This type of thinking can be referred to as "calculative thinking" or "rational choice" (Winter and May 2001). In this case the monetary benefits of compliance outweigh the monetary losses. For instance, agreement may open up new markets or avoid a heavy fine. A *social motive* earns the firm approval from its constituents. Perhaps it is asked to cease production of a dangerous toy or to improve its environmental stewardship. This may gain the firm positive press and accolades for its contribution to societal well-being (which Ellickson refers to as "social welfare"). Finally, a *moral motive* concerns a firm's desire to "do the right thing" and conform as requested (Neilsen and Parker 2012).

Acceptance is voluntary and enforcement is passive, with only education and awareness of the regulatory situation. This informal way of regulation may be in the regulator's culture or may be a response to the target's extent of agreement (Groot and Merchant 2000). Informal control may also be exerted when agreement is not reached on implementation of the required regulations. In this situation there is often much persuasion of the target to respond in a positive way.

A lack of agreement seems to motivate the formal control mode where a prosecution orientation results in management via principles of command-and-control. In such cases, even when the target of control agrees with the regulations, they may or may not implement them. The regulator may respond with threats and attempts to frighten the target of control (Hawkins 1984). By-the-book conformance is demanded of the target, and fines and even imprisonment are on the table. In short, agreement is an important determinant of control mechanisms in use, which we will discuss later in more detail.

Do regulatory actions work?

It appears that whether regulatory actions work or not may depend on the perspective of the regulator, the target of regulation, and the many constituents of both, including the general public. Who's to say what cost should be put on child welfare, consumer safety, financial oversight, or workplace safety? Given that, we can only examine the cost tradeoff and consumer reactions on the effectiveness and efficiency of success on individual and unique situations (Grabosky 1995).

Some researchers in this area have tried to determine the success of regulatory actions, although there is little common view on definitions, measurement, and a nomology for success. What is clear is that some form of intervention is required when compliance is not automatic and straightforward (Braithwaite 2007). On the independent variable side, we might summarize this investigation as the effects of positive vs. negative sanctions. We may further delineate rewards and punishments by mode, formal (command and control, deterrence) and informal. On the dependent variable side, May (2005) suggests the examination of client resistance to regulatory attempts (fighting back), consistency and fairness, and reduced corruption.

Do formal control sanctions work? Deterrence theory suggests that targets of control are rational actors and will take opportunities to increase profit when possible. The reaction to non-compliance in this case consists of very specific, narrow, and uniform rules that clearly state the rights and wrongs of the target's options for response. When formal monitoring mechanisms report that response is not in order, threats of punishments and enacted punishments — such as fines — are to be applied. In that sense, control works. However, an additional objective of regulatory control is to rehabilitate the transgressor. Job *et al.* (2007) report that rehabilitation may only have a short-term effect at best, at the cost of the possible delegitimization of the agency's authority for its heavy-handed approach. In contrast to this mandatory approach to regulation is the voluntary approach (May 2005), which is seen as a more informal type of control.

Do informal control sanctions work? Although agencies have traditionally relied upon formal and negative sanctions (Grabosky 1995), an alternative to the formal command and control approach is the consideration of a cooperative, more voluntary compliance approach (Job *et al.* 2007; May 2005). This approach suggests the target of control perceives a "sense of duty to adhere to the rules" (May 2005, p. 33). Organizations are more likely to respond positively to interactive education and training programs, staff performance assessments, grants, subsidies, tax credits, loan guarantees, praise, research and development funding, and recruitment assistance programs than rude or abusive deterrence methods. After all, it is human nature that rewards typically work better than punishments; is that the case in the regulatory environment as well (Braithwaite 2002)?

The delineation between formal and informal, command and deterrence and voluntary, is rather fuzzy. They are often offered in combination to varying degrees, so it is difficult to separate individual effects. Results are also in conflict with one another: while Grabosky (1995) is emphatic that punishment doesn't work, May (2005) shows that mandatory compliance methods are more successful than voluntary compliance when it comes to gaining commitment to adopt regulation. Finally, Gilliland and Manning (2002) find that informal control mechanisms (advice, rich communication, education) are more effective than formal control mechanisms (rigid administration of the rules) at both gaining compliance and reducing opportunistic behaviors.

A final example of third-party, network-based control considers a coalition of organizations that work together toward a common goal. High-technology research consortiums sometimes band together to ward off foreign firm penetration, or intruders from another industry. Japanese *keiretsus* take this concept to another level. A *keiretsu* is an informal collection of firms that help one another by exchanging employees, management skills, or other support with one another. The usual *keiretsu* may include a financial institution, an electronics producer, a heavy equipment manufacturer, and an information technology firm. Typically, there are no ownership stakes, just a sharing of goodwill and support.

Discussion: Networks as Third-Party Control

A final important area considering the third-party control system is found in the channels of distribution literature. Here, networks of multiple firms work together to distribute products and services through a marketing channel to end-user consumers or firms. Consider a Supplier → Distributor → Retailer network, as is common in the electronics and grocery industries. Here, the supplier must control the distributor and try to control the retailer through influence over the distributor. Thus, the supplier plays the role of the third-party controller. Research in this area is sparse. However, network researchers think that the supplier's dealings with the retailer also have effects on the distributor. For instance, should representatives of the supplier visit their retail accounts they may try to confirm whether the distributor is providing effective service to the retailer. Thus, in this case, control, or maybe weak control, is not necessarily tied to the transaction, but more to the relationship. Also, the supplier's dealings with the distributor have effects on the retailer. Although interesting, the relationships may also be explained by the power-dependence model. The supplier exerts power — although likely via different bases of power — which give it the license to influence the distributor via the retailer. Typical network theories include TCE (Kim *et al.* 2011, Wathne and Heide 2004), social network theory (Shipilov and Li 2012, Wuyts *et al.* 2004), and institutional theory (McFarland *et al.* 2008).

Chapter 7

A General Hypothesis and the Costs of Control

In this chapter, we continue to build on our theory of social control by addressing the costs of control and how these costs determine the control structures in use. From this we derive our general control hypothesis. We begin by asking, "What must be accomplished in order to attain control?" This is not simple, as one party's idea of control may be very different from another's.

Whether control works or not is somewhat dependent on our outcome variables of choice. A common description of an acceptable control outcome is an increase in compliance. Another is a decrease in opportunism. Let's discuss both.

First, compliance occurs when the target bends to the controller's will and accepts the proposed terms of the request. This may mean conforming to a law or regulation despite not being attitudinally on board with it. Thus, compliance, *per se*, is a behavioral construct that only considers the result of the control *attempt*, not the *outcomes* of performing as requested. Further, as we know, firms respond quite differently because of compliance. Some will truly conform, and others will conform and retaliate. We can expect the same thing in a dyadic or self-control setting.

But while compliance may rest at the heart of control, there is much more to control than compliance. It seems that control is in the eye of the beholder. Firm A may impose control mechanisms on its target merely to get it to do what A requires. That is, compliance is enough; it is not interested in developing a deeper relationship with the target. Consider Firm B, which not only may want specific conformance to its requirements but to also develop a longer-term relationship with its target, including the relational norms that go along with that. Perhaps it proposes informal controls while ignoring the written contract in hopes of developing a trusting situation (much like Gary Bell and Kawasaki). Finally consider Firm C, which wants to start a strategic relationship with its target to motivate a long-term partnership via the investments of credible commitments. The potential partners are concerned about long-term orientation, aligned goals, and investments; what happens in the day-to-day relationship is not as important as aligning the long term. Although compliance itself may be similar in all three cases, the goals of control are quite different. Clearly, a typical perspective on compliance only tells part of the story.

If we expand our notion of compliance to consider more than conforming to rules, we can speak of control mechanisms' ability to align relationships both attitudinally and behaviorally. Inventory, logistics, marketing programs, and policies must all be aligned among firms in terms of timing, location, and price. Such alignment among partnering firms means that the daily work is getting done and the firms are reaping the economic benefits of the relationship.

But there is surely more to alignment than coordinating physical tasks. When attitudes and intentions are motivated in one party's control mechanisms the focus shifts from the here and now to the longer term. Aligned attitudes can mean mutual intentions on safeguarding and maintaining the relationship (Ganesan 1994). This is the case in many buyer–seller and channels of distribution relationships.

Finally, let us consider a strong form of control, the alignment of credible commitments (Anderson and Weitz 1992). Mutual investments bond firms together by aligning their incentives. Such investments tie the parties together and form the basis of a continuing relationship.

Thus, alignment can take place at different levels of magnitude. The controller can motivate compliance in terms of tasks, attitudes, and specific investments. Our suggestion is quite bold, control rules in formal and/or informal modes can tie firms together in the short term, moderate term, and long term. It can do so at the task, attitudinal, and investment levels.

Regarding opportunism, we can array its different forms on a continuum from what we might call "less to greater severity." Using the types of opportunism from Wathne and Heide (2000), we suggest the following (see Figure 7.1).

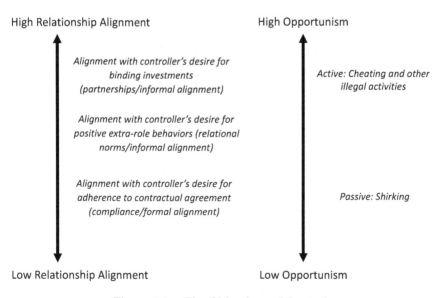

High Relationship Alignment   High Opportunism

Alignment with controller's desire for binding investments (partnerships/informal alignment)

Active: Cheating and other illegal activities

Alignment with controller's desire for positive extra-role behaviors (relational norms/informal alignment)

Alignment with controller's desire for adherence to contractual agreement (compliance/formal alignment)

Passive: Shirking

Low Relationship Alignment   Low Opportunism

Figure 7.1. The Objectives of Control

The continuum suggests two extremes of opportunism, one that is within the law (also known as passive or weak form opportunism) and one that implies immoral or illegal behavior (also known as active or strong form opportunism).

Passive opportunism considers the legal case of cheating, where the target of control refuses to (1) adapt to new contracts as conditions change, (2) invest in the partner as expected, or, (3) perform as agreed. As we know by now, agents only act if profitable. Thus, they are often very proficient at actively selling the supplier's brand. They reap immediate rewards in terms of margins, and they often look good under output monitoring, but there is more to the story. There is more to selling than the act of selling, such as training, market development, and performing after-sales service. Such activities are often difficult to monitor, so as Hechter might ask, "Why spend time on it?" In fact, in strict agency terms, it would be irrational to do so. In such a case, the agent is not cooking the books, stealing, or intentionally booby-trapping the relationship, merely free-riding. This can also be thought of as "passive representation" (Gilliland and Kim 2014) where the agent officially represents the line, but does so with absolute minimal effort. Passive representation is overlooked and often dangerous because the principal may not detect that the agent is not performing, it just knows that sales are down. The agent may blame the market, the environment, the competition, or even the principal, but not itself.

Active opportunism involves specific actions taken by the target that are deemed illegal and immoral. Cheating on expense reports, fudging numbers, taking unauthorized discounts, territory violations, and misrepresentation are more extreme in nature, and constitute a crossing of the moral boundary.

The solutions and causes of opportunism are complex, but I suggest that opportunism can be positively driven by inappropriate control behaviors and effectively managed by formal and informal controls, such as incentives, monitoring, and trust.

A General Hypothesis

What does control look like? We've done a quite thorough job of outlining the specifics of the mechanisms used to motivate the target's compliance and alignment (e.g., setting standards, monitoring, sanctioning), but what does it *look like*? That is, what rules of control will be used in any particular control action, and further, who will make this decision? Will one, two, or all three control systems be activated at the same time? Will the mechanisms be used in their formal or informal modes? Can both formal and informal modes be used simultaneously? It's amazingly complex, and there are an infinite number of combinations that may describe control of a single circumstance. Conceptualizing such a beast makes you want to throw your hands up in frustration, but let's see if we can at least get a handle on why control looks like it does.

Based on an economic rationale, Ellickson (1987) suggests that the costs of control dictate the system, mode, and resultant mechanisms of control that are used to guide and manage the relationship. Or, as Gilliland (2023) suggests, control mechanisms are applied to reduce the costs of maintaining control. If it is highly costly to rely on formal standards and contracts, an informal mechanism that serves a similar purpose will be developed. If formal outcome or behavioral monitoring is too costly or unavailable, relational monitoring (the clan) will assume control (see Ouchi 1979). The reverse also applies. If it is too time-consuming and expensive to build trust in a relationship, formal mechanisms may be applied.

More formally, we can write a general hypothesis of control that states,

A particular combination of control systems, modes, and mechanisms will be implemented to gain a desired level of relationship alignment while minimizing the controller's total costs of control.

Such a simple hypothesis for such complex combinations of possibilities warrants further explanation. Let's address a few key points.

First, we should be quite clear that the costs under consideration, at this stage of the process, belong to the organization attempting control: For instance, if a new monitoring scheme is necessary, the decision to implement is in the hands of the controller, thus it is the controller's costs that are considered. Also considered are the controller's benefits of the new scheme. In a more bilateral effort, perhaps the controller has a unique cost of building and maintaining trust in the relationship. Again, the costs that count are the controller's costs as it builds its control scheme.

Second, any given control situation will be managed by self-control, dyadic control, or third-party control: Managers themselves may take personal actions to maintain a relationship, or to end one. Managers' teams may be instructed to act in a similar fashion, where the culture of the relationship and closeness of the management team may move to improve the dyadic relationship or terminate the relationship. Dyadic control suggests that firms may extend across the boundaries of the relationship to control or participate in mutual control solutions with the partner. Also, on witnessing certain actions in its purview, an outside third party (regulator or trade association) may step in to alter, advise, or guide the situation. General formal or informal modes, depending on costs, will emerge to ensure the relationship stays on track or is expanded, attenuated, or terminated. Within such modes, the specific mechanisms of control will guide the day-by-day management of the relationship.

Third, the degree of control attempted is not fixed, but dependent on the extent of the controller's desire to align the relationship: Regarding a suitable level of control, different relationships, with different goals and concerns require different levels, or types, of control. Organizations that work together in a highly non-integrated fashion (think international exporting), require little control by the exporter over the importer's needs for input. The importer already knows the market, its customer base, and how to market to it. On the other hand, two large firms engaged in a joint venture will require more severe alignment as they navigate their complexities. Thus, for each situation, the requirements for control vary. Some situations may require a formal, tight controlling process, and others a less formal, looser process. Thus, given the control situation required, control modes and mechanisms will be adjusted to fit the need.

Fourth, complexities arise when multiple controllers are involved: Multiple controllers may take the form of different control systems and the actors' relationships in the control setting. Each independent actor may wish to control, share control, or be controlled. Thus, the type of control *desired* is important from each controller's perspective. Firm A may decide that informal control is an adequate mode of control, given the situation, however, Firm B may opt for more formal mechanisms. For each, they will attempt the lowest-cost form of control, *each from its own perspective.*

Because the hypothesis dictates the least expensive form of control, one may wonder why this isn't always an informal control solution. As mentioned above, informal control allows shortcuts around formal transactions-based exchange. There are three reasons which dictate the existence of formal control as either the guiding form of control or as part of a formal/informal combination of control mechanisms. First, in many situations, *formal control mechanisms are irreplaceable*. An informal legal-backed remedy is not available, or rarely available, when it comes to employment contracts, industrial purchasing agreements, production details, distribution agreements, supply chain margins, financial arrangements, asset ownership, and many other circumstances. For instance, although psychological contracts exist, they lay on top of, or fill holes in, written contracts. Without written, formal agreements, firms would be unable to safeguard assets from risky conditions. Second, *formal controls may be required in low control situations*. In low control situations (again, the international exporter), it is too costly to formally structure a highly aligned relationship (Bello 2011). Geographic and cultural distances prohibit the necessary exchange to even attempt to control in a substantive manner, thus formal control, even a skeleton version of formal control, may be required. Third, *informal controls have costs too,* such as relationship building, which relies on the use of informal control mechanisms and norm development. In a seminal article, Dwyer *et al.* (1987) explained the formation, development, management, and dissolution of a relationship. They stress how there are many false starts in finding and beginning to bond with a partner, including a lack of trust and a fear of being cheated upon. There are trial phases to relationships when norms begin to take over from one-on-one transactions, and many mistakes and misunderstandings at this stage, which may get in the way of developing a smooth, low-cost bond. Also difficult is the notion of maintaining the relationship. They point out that "social bonds tend to weaken and dissolve unless actively maintained" (p. 19). This constant maintenance takes time and continued investments into the partner. Such investments include the investments of specific assets as the partners get to know one another's products, markets, and ways of doing business. Obviously, these investments, or credible commitments, come with the potential for transaction costs, exposures to loss, and the need for asset safeguarding (Anderson and Weitz 1992). All of these are a drag on the savings created from the use of informal control mechanisms. Finally, there are many environmental, industry, and relationship conditions, which require the use of formal modes and mechanisms. These will be discussed subsequently. Again, although formal control seems inevitable in any transaction, informal control may or may not be part of the solution.

The Costs of Control

The costs of control are the costs, both economic and social, of aligning the relationship. The costs of control are drawn directly from the mechanisms and modes of control that are needed to maintain or return the control condition to a desired alignment. While the mechanisms that are applied can be many, authors have generally accepted the fact that the low-cost solution is implemented. That is, the various modes and combinations of methods suggest an optimal mixed solution (Ellickson 1987). But just what are these various costs that accompany control? A more micro view is examined as follows.

Costs of control = net costs of compliance
+ net costs of informal alignment
+ value of social welfare
+ deadweight costs

The net costs of compliance are generally the benefits gained to the controller from compliance minus the costs of formal control applied that are adequate to gain compliance. Formal control is applied to decrease the variance of behaviors and actions that produce high costs of transactions. Their resultant costs arise that reflect the overall costs of managing the transaction. These costs include, first, the *costs of setting formal standards.*

These are costs such as those of negotiating, writing, haggling over, and modifying the contract or written agreement on which the transaction operates (Dahlstrom and Nygaard 1999). Other costs that must be considered are the costs of financial directives, memos, rules that guide the relationship, and formal statements that describe the expectations of the exchange. As transactions become more complex, the costs of contracts rise. However, well-specified contracts reduce the probabilities of risk and encourage trust and cooperation. They may also encourage long-term relationships by increasing the penalties that accompany early exit. Overall costs are reduced in terms of opportunistic behaviors, handling anticipated contingencies, executing standard procedures, and meeting quality standards. Also, communication will be smoother and information asymmetries will reduce (Zaheer *et al.* 1998).

Second, the *net costs of formal monitoring* include the costs of running the surveillance system such as establishing outcome and behavioral measures, engaging in complex verification processes, and confirming results (Dahlstrom and Nygaard 1999). These are considered in relation to the benefits gained from monitoring. Also included are efforts to bring performance back into alignment with standards and expectations, which may result in punishment costs. As discussed previously, the monitoring of outcomes is typically considered a rational based, more formal, oversight system, where performance is judged solely on how much is produced. A behavioral-based monitoring process is aligned with more transformation-based information and more prescriptive guidance for employees or agents (Ouchi 1979, Ouchi and Maguire 1975).

Third, the *net costs of formal sanctioning* include the benefits of formal incentives and formal punishments as accrued to the controller minus its costs of implementation. The formal costs of incentives are the expenses to motivate and encourage employees, intermediaries, and partners to perform as expected by the controller. These include forms of remuneration such as salaries, bonuses, commissions, margins, subjective support programs, decreased interest rates offered to partners on borrowed funds (e.g., floor plans), and other ways of motivation. Traditionally, in discussing salaries vs. commissions, the percentage of total compensation of salaries is more closely aligned to formal, vertically integrated structures, whereas commissions are more closely aligned to nonintegrated, less formal, market-based approaches (Bergen *et al.* 1992, Dahlstrom and Nygaard 1999, Klein *et al.* 1989, Oliver and Anderson 1994).

Unfortunately, there are other costs associated with incentives which are less easy to identify and account for. Benabou and Tirole (2003) describe how incentives may be a weak enforcer over time due to the hidden costs of rewards. These hidden costs result in a drag on the motivation system, requiring more funds to motivate at the same or a lesser level. More specifically, hidden costs come in the form of explicit incentives crowding out the intrinsic motivation that comes with the satisfaction of a task well done. That is, that the higher the extrinsic incentive, the less the intrinsic motivation. Also, such extrinsic rewards may damage the quality performance that comes with intrinsic motivation. These costs must also be considered. On the other hand, incentive costs are typically much less than the benefits accrued form a strong incentives plan. Besides the revenue generated from sales, goodwill is established with partners, which leads to less expensive trusting relationships and the earning of social welfare.

The costs of punishments consider expenses related to enforcing the contract. When contractual obligations are not met, or the firms do not adequately adapt to one another the controller may be forced to realign the offending behaviors to those established in the contract (Dahlstrom and Nygaard 1999). These may be real costs in terms of lawsuits, firings, and demotions, or the costs of conflict and retaliations (e.g., Hibbard and Stern 2001). Conflict and retaliation costs may be severe and even lead to lost relationships.

Regarding the net costs of informal alignment, the formal costs of control are necessary in any inter-organizational relationship in order to initiate and maintain transactions. However, informal "shortcuts" to control have been recognized for many years (Macaulay 1963). Such informal handshake agreements allow less need to use, negotiate, and enforce formal contracts and to extensively monitor all transactions. Formal control is often avoided due to the transaction costs associated with implementing formal mechanisms (Ellickson 1991), thus, in some cases, informal controls can support the relationship.

Cost reductions due to the use of informal control mechanisms are considered *relational rents* by Dyer and Singh (1998). Relational rents are cost savings due to the existence and continuation of the ongoing relationship. These cost savings come in several forms. First, transaction costs decrease because of the shortcuts and informal agreements mentioned above. These amount to potentially extraordinary savings due to the reductions in negotiating, haggling, writing, and enforcing the relationship. These are replaced with informal standard setting, monitoring, and sanctioning. There is less of a bureaucratic base needed for informal control mechanisms because transactions rely on a social base. Second, firms are motivated to maintain such a relationship, implying they will curb their shirking and opportunistic behaviors. Formal control mechanisms do not need to be implemented as often to keep the parties on track and focused on the business at hand. Third, self-enforcing mechanisms, such as bilateral goal monitoring are more effective than intrusive monitoring because self-enforcing mechanisms maximize the creation of value within the relationship. They also reduce the direct costs of monitoring. Fourth, the partners expect profits to be fairly divided, also reducing the costs of haggling. Fifth, agreements and contracts can be adjusted on the fly without having to endure time-consuming negotiations. This allows partners to be more nimble to dynamic threats in the short term. Finally, a key part of any informal relationship is the frequency of communications and the sharing of information. Cannon and Homburg (2000) find that increases in the various forms of communication (e.g., face-to-face, telephone, written, and electronic) reduce product and operations costs between business partners.

Cost savings may also accrue as *social welfare* is created. When considering how norms emerge among groups, Ellickson states, "members of a close-knit group develop and maintain social norms whose content serves to maximize the aggregate welfare that members attain in their workaday affairs with one another" (1991, p. 167). In other words, people and organizations in informal, egalitarian settings have an ongoing need to create satisfactory outcomes. Although this is a subjective assessment of the advantages of norm-sharing, using an objective system to measure individual satisfaction is potentially unreliable. Nevertheless, social welfare is produced with the associated efficiencies and rents created by partners' workday affairs, which include simple day-to-day business operations. Control costs are reduced as paperwork is replaced with personal conversations, complex contracts are put in file drawers with little need for consultation, unanticipated changes to the business landscape are met with mutual recognition and action, and future planning is enthusiastically shared among the close-knit group. Social welfare increases with satisfaction, and satisfaction has been linked to positive situations such as cooperation, trust, commitment, and non-coercive bargaining (Geyskens *et al.* 1999) — all more efficient and informal ways of doing business. Thus, it seems quite clear that informal control mechanisms produce more satisfactory outcomes than formal controls.

Social welfare also considers the full network of constituents to the exchange in question. As day-to-day operations are streamlined, low-cost solutions are created and such savings may be passed on through the network or up and down the supply chain or distribution channel. Also, consider a regulator or powerful trade association which convinces an industry to produce cleaner, safer, and more sustainable product solutions. Satisfaction and social welfare may affect very large numbers of constituents.

Finally, deadweight costs are the opportunity costs associated with relationship minimization or even disintegration. Future transactions and deals will not be realized, leaving lost opportunities for revenue and growth. Deadweight costs are also important in that they act as a signpost to direct the parties to engage in business instead of suffering these costs (Ellickson 1991).

Discussion: At What Cost Compliance?

If the point of control is compliance, one must ask, "At what cost, compliance"? First, from the formal side, compliance means a forced acquiescence. Compliance will likely occur when forced, but there may be serious repercussions, which begs our question. Clearly, a great deal of positive comes from compliance from the controller's side. But it takes participation from both sides in a business partnership, so one may wonder what gets lost.

One thing lost may be the spirit of the partnership. Forced compliance invites backlash in several forms. Opportunism occurs as firms feel taken advantage of, causing additional and costly safeguarding mechanisms on the side of the controller. A particular form of opportunism, shirking, may be particularly nefarious. Shirking pays off for controlees when their slacking behavior evades the controller's monitoring system. A key problem with shirking in this case is that the controller doesn't realize it is occurring. Shirking intermediaries passively represent the supplier by holding inventory on its lot and aggressively selling competing products. When questioned on a lack of performance they may give excuses such as the price is too high, the competition is ferocious, or there are product quality problems. Retaliation occurs as well when partners feel cheated. This often results in the need for additional safeguards and even relationship dissolution. At the least, there is reduced cooperation among parties.

Informal controls can make compliance more worthwhile by reducing costs via norms, trust, long-term orientation, and relationalism. Still, norms take a long and costly time to build and trust often invites opportunistic behaviors should the controller drop its guard. So, what may be a key factor in determining the advantage of compliance may be the social goodwill that results. This goodwill, or satisfaction, is difficult to quantify of course, but it may pervade the relationship, particularly when we consider end-use customers or other constituents of control. Perhaps that is what makes compliance worth the cost.

Chapter 8

Control Structure

In this chapter, we revisit some previously discussed, extant models of control and our general control framework. Then, we build a proposed model of control based on the modes of control discussed earlier. In discussing these formal and informal modes, we rely primarily on the dyadic control literature as this is where most of the research has been conducted. By the end of the chapter, we will have discussed how the costs of control determine the control mechanisms in use, including combinations of control. Finally, we will discuss the internal and external drivers of costs and control structures.

The first topic for consideration is whether control emerges over time or whether control is designed and implemented by managers. Clearly, process models of relationship formation, continuance, and dissolution exist in several literature (e.g., Dwyer *et al.* 1987, Ring and Van de Ven 1994). In general, relationships tend to start in a transactional fashion with little need to bond. Relationships are expensive to start and maintain, thus firms tend to begin with small orders, small expectations, and hands-off relationships. As time progresses, bonds form and relationships tend to emerge. Relationships can take the form of specific investments, mutual planning and decision-making, and the growth of trust between the partners. Both contract-based and self-enforcing safeguards protect specific assets and allow the actors to set longer-term horizons to the relationship. Eventually, the relationship is controlled by a mutuality of intentions supported by written expectations. Thus, relationships grow and decline over time. Does control follow a similar pattern? Researchers believe so. Control certainly involves implementing the specific tools required to move the relationship forward. In distribution relationships, boilerplate contracts exist that specify incentive programs, monitoring processes, and punishment and correction schemes. Many of these contracts are eventually modified to reflect changes and idiosyncrasies in relationships. In franchise arrangements, the boilerplates are seldom negotiated and are laden with a power advantage toward the franchisor. In many business-to-business relationships contracts set standards for framing the transactions that start the relationships. Thus, control is implemented.

However, as Mallen (1973) would suggest, channel control changes over time depending on a variety of characteristics with the relationship and the environment. As dependencies in relationships change, the responsibilities of the partners change via *functional spin-off*, as actors re-sort who does what. Thus, it is suggested that as arrangements deal with contingencies a channel may expand or contract, implying necessary modifications in how relationships are controlled. Resellers may take on new functions or spin-off functions that are no longer feasible. Layers of channel resellers may emerge (say, wholesalers) and require the implementation of new contracts that cause a series of changes with other intermediaries.

But control relationships also change on an individual scale over time due to the formation of norms, trust, and more specific contracts. Both bilateral and unilateral control processes work together to provide control structures. That is, formal control mechanisms tend to remain in place (even though some specifics may be ignored), even as informal mechanisms emerge from the relationship. Thus, control structures can be planned, but change naturally over time to respond to new situations and requirements.

A second consideration is whether control can reach an equilibrium condition where control modes and mechanisms are stable over a considerable amount of time. Not according to van der Kolk *et al.* (2020). Equilibrium requires a sense of stability, and interorganizational exchange is fluid. From a layman's standpoint, control changes almost daily; new contracts, new incentive schemes, new information from ongoing monitoring processes, etc. Of course, these can be considered micro changes, but what about the changing of control modes (formal to informal or the reverse) or the emergence of a combined mode? At what point does the manager decide to not refer to contracts, and base assessments on other information, such as intentions and effort, conversation, goals, and trust? To understand this process, we need a basis for understanding what determines control modes and how they might be modified, intentionally or unintentionally.

We have already established that there are two modes of control, formal and informal. Formal control is based on strict interpretations of contracts and agreements, where compliance with the contract is a necessity for a useful, coordinated relationship. The mechanisms of formal control include the writing of specific standards of behavior in contracts and agreements, formalized monitoring of processes or output, and formalized sanctions of performance, either positive (incentives) or negative (punishments) in nature. However, although formal control mechanisms are identified in studies of TCA, many governance structures are incompatible with a TCA conceptualization (Ebers and Oerlemans 2016). They, and others, suggest that a formal perspective on control represents an *under-socialized* view of exchange. Such a view suggests little need for formal adaptations and formal administrative controls. Another mode of control, informal control, occurs when firms come together and trust one another, collaborate with one another, and value their reputations over strict monetary gains. Although informal control is based on such agreements, like-mindedness, trust and other informal, and social-based conditions exist. The standards are established based on the culture of the relationship, industry norms, and everyday activities. Informal monitoring of the standards is based on shared goals, self-analysis, and a determination of whether the intentions of relationship length are shared among the parties.

Thus, formal and informal control are clearly part of every relationship, but how do they work together? How do they combine?

The Primary Drivers of Control Structure

If control structures are based on cost and social welfare, we should discuss the drivers of those important issues. In doing so, we address the question of how control is motivated, and why it is different from situation to situation. The areas that we shall discuss include the disposition of the relationship between or within organizations, the behaviors of the actors involved in the exchange, industry norms, and risk. Importantly, I suggest that these drivers of control change the costs of the mechanisms in some way. By changing the mechanisms' costs it makes it more or less likely to be used in the final control structure. For a graphic depiction see Figure 8.1.

Relationship disposition

Relationship disposition refers to the relationship between organizations, firms, and even individuals that are involved in the exchange. All transactions have economic and social bases (Bouillon *et al.* 2006, Granovetter 1985), and these are reflected in the ability and desire of firms to work together to smooth transaction costs and foster long-lasting relationships.

Goal Congruence: It is the sharing of common goals. Firms that share goals tend to have an endless relationship horizon, or at least a long-term relationship horizon (Ganesan 1994, Ring and Van de Ven 1994).

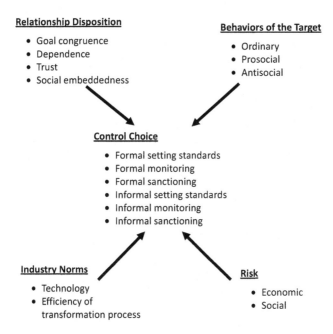

Figure 8.1.   Cost Drivers of Control Structure

Generally speaking, goal sharing usually implies that the organizations have a desire to maintain the relationship. This tends to be accompanied by relational norms that drive the exchange toward mutually beneficial solutions.

Regarding the economic benefits of shared goals, Bouillon *et al.* (2006) examined differences in agency (goals not shared) and stewardship (goals shared) theories. They found that resource accumulation, volume of services provided, operating efficiency, and cost-structure flexibility all improved with a stewardship model. Similarly, Gilliland and Kim (2014) found positive relationships when typical agents agreed with the strategic goals of the principal.

However, it is not necessarily the case that goal alignment means relationalism. In a regulatory setting, Gilliland and Manning (2002) found that mere acceptance of the role of the regulator by the regulated firm was sufficient to change both the control foundation of the controller and the actions of the firm under control. Agreement with the regulator's role implied that the firm understands and supports why the rules of control are as they are. In this case, it meant that the controlled firm believed in the food safety regulations on which they were being evaluated. Thus, accepting the role of the controller implies that the target validates its actions and behaviors. Role acceptance was found to be associated positively with informal control attempts by the regulator and negatively associated with formal control attempts.

Dependence: The importance of power and dependence on organizational and interorganizational relationships cannot be overestimated. Power, which we described earlier as a "license to control," is determinant in driving lock-in, switching costs, attitudinal and credible commitments, costs, many other key elements of relationships, and their success or failure (e.g., Anderson and Weitz 1992, Buchanan 1992; Jackson 1985). From a control standpoint, the more power Firm A holds over Firm B, the more likely it is to have successful control capabilities. The more dependent firm (in this case Firm B) is considered the firm under control. Two other situations include mutual control, where there may be very little mutual dependence among A and B (thus, little to control) or a great deal of mutual dependence among A and B.

As described in Table 8.1, the extent that dependence adds to or detracts from a firm's costs of control is a function of the control mechanism in question and the dependence situation. There are several cases where dependence contributes to control costs in a substantive way:

- *Setting Standards*: When A is dependent on B (either on its own or mutually), the situation may change as the relationship gets more complex and grows at either the requirement of B or due to mutual agreement from both parties. Either way, contractual changes are necessary as A negotiates for more favorable terms.

Table 8.1. Control Cost Contributions Based on Relative Dependence

| Scenario* | Standards | Monitoring | Sanctions | | Deadweight Losses |
			Incentives	Punishments	
A* High B Low	High as it tries to negotiate more favorable terms	High as it tries to fight opportunism	Moderate as it offers better terms	Low as it has no power to punish	Very high as it can't access adequate alternatives
A* Low B High	Low as there is no need to change standards	Moderate to ensure compliance	Moderate to maintain B's extrinsic motivation	High to keep B in line when it wants to leave	Low; it can leave if it wants
A* Low B Low (Mutual)	Low as there are few requirements for standards	Low	Low	Low	Low
A* High B High (Mutual)	High as relationship evolves standards change	Moderate as relationship is guided by trust and norms	High to motivate extrinsic and intrinsic motivation	Low as there is little need to punish the partner	Moderate as there are alternatives that may not be needed

Note: *In terms of A's relative dependence on B.

- *Monitoring*: When A is dependent on B, B is much more liable to opportunistic attempts, therefore it must constantly keep watch on its partner to ensure that shirking and opportunism are not prevalent.
- *Incentives*: When A and B are mutually dependent on one another in a substantive way, there are both economic and social dimensions to the relationship. To support economic motivation, extrinsic incentives must be available to return financial gains to the relationship. To support social motivation, intrinsic incentives must also be available. Thus, a high level of high- and low-powered incentives must drive the relationship for both firms.
- *Punishments*: Dependent firms have no license to punish, but more powerful firms do. If A has power over B it must use sanctions to keep B from leaving the relationship, or, more likely, from cheating to stay in the relationship.
- *Deadweight Losses*: The more a firm is relatively dependent on another, its options narrow because it cannot leave the current relationship for a new opportunity. Thus, a highly dependent firm may miss out on many alternative relationships because they cannot be accessed. This greatly increases deadweight costs. To make matters worse, there is no corresponding reduction in control costs (as, for instance, monitoring would reduce opportunism), it is purely a loss.

To illustrate the complexities of control, different permutations of dependence and control costs are provided in the table.

Trust: It is a key element in any control relationship, and there are additional control savings due to the existence of trust. Trust complements most any form of control (Gulati and Nickerson 2008) as it reduces the barriers to informal exchange, and thus, the costs associated with formal control. Trust is a self-enforcing safeguard (Dyer and Singh 1998) that mitigates contracting hazards, lowering the overall costs of the transaction. Trust produces more common understandings that fill holes in contracts and guard against the possibilities of opportunistic behaviors (Zaheer *et al.* 1998). More specifically, trust reduces the costs of setting standards by reducing the costs of negotiation (Zaheer *et al.* 1998), which allows agreements to be reached more quickly. There is less haggling when the parties trust that they will both receive a fair distribution of income. Monitoring costs are reduced because there is less need for verification and fewer meetings (Fang *et al.* 2008, Selnes and Sallis 2003). Also, less monitoring is needed because trust mitigates asymmetries in information by allowing more open and honest sharing of information. Trust also reduces the scope, intensity, and frequency of dysfunctional conflict.

Trust is a more effective and less costly alternative to both contracts and vertical integration, thus improving performance outcomes (Heide and John 1990, Zaheer *et al.* 1998, Zaheer and Venkatraman 1995). It is typically aligned with informal control because, "partners are likely to use less formal governance when there is trust between them" (Gulati and Nickerson 2008, p. 689).

Although trust lowers the costs of transactions, we must also consider that trust has its own set of costs. Recent work on the dark side of bonded relationships (Lumineau 2017, Villena *et al.* 2011) indicates that trust itself may create cost problems. Those willing to trust automatically let their guards down because monitoring itself is not needed. Instead, trusting managers assume that they are not being cheated and that all is well. When performance is not verified in some way, the partner opens itself to opportunistic behaviors which has its own set of costs (Gundlach and Cannon 2010).

Social Embeddedness: This concerns the extent that the economic transaction is wrapped in a social context. This suggests that all transactions, at least theoretically, have formal cost-reducing elements within the exchange. That is, the higher the degree of social elements in a transaction, the greater the reductions of formal costs in the exchange. The social elements of the exchange minimize opportunism while increasing efficiencies of the relationship between partners and reducing formal costs such as the costs of contracting, administering, and monitoring. This is done via closer, smoother social interactions which increase efficiencies, all while maximizing the shared values and satisfaction in the relationship.

Behaviors of the target

An actor's behaviors can be classified as ordinary, antisocial, or prosocial. Each has specific implications for the costs of compliance (see Figure 8.2).

Ordinary Behaviors: Ordinary behavior is the regular and ongoing behavior that maintains a relationship. It is how business is executed every day. Agents (and principals) perform as their jobs were designed, guided by the contract, distribution agreement, or simply normative ties or ways of doing business. A key issue is that the principal, sometimes accompanied by the agent, designs the agent's job to earn normal returns for the partnership (Holmstrom and Milgrom 1991). Ordinary behaviors are driven by formal incentive and compensation plans that control both specific tasks identified and unobserved tasks necessary for success (Lo *et al.* 2011). The development of normal expectations and social ties demonstrates that small groups of people cooperate on an informal basis without the threat of legal sanctions.

This within-role behavior is typically covered in the standard operating agreement or contract. Ordinary behavior can be evaluated as positive (e.g., carrying out typical marketing tasks) or negative (e.g., failing to meet objectives, shirking, or violating the agreement in some way; Gilliland 2023). Standard incentives and sanctions provide the motivation, reward, and punishment as outlined in the operating agreement, and the system runs itself requiring no specific

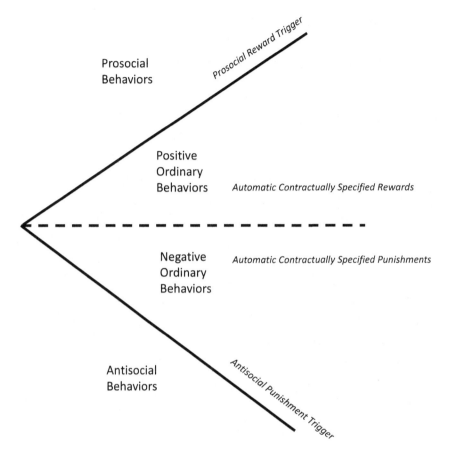

Figure 8.2. Behaviors and Control Triggers

interventions. When positive results are achieved, standard incentives are paid per the contract. Ordinary behaviors that do not achieve positive results trigger the need to examine the specific behaviors committed and consider how to bring the relationship back into alignment as desired by the controller. Because ordinary behaviors are framed as formal control behaviors (Gilliland 2023), there is typically little addition to the costs of the exchange besides the paying of additional incentives for positive performance. However, negative ordinary behaviors also add to the costs of control because punishments may be accompanied by managerial wrangling and conflict.

At the positive and negative boundaries of ordinary behavior are response triggers that trip when the agent crosses the line into either antisocial or prosocial behaviors (as perceived by the principal). *Response triggers* are sanctions that activate the social control system by, typically, either punishing the agent for crossing the boundary into antisocial behavior or rewarding the agent for crossing the boundary into prosocial behavior.[1] Importantly, the triggers are set based on the principal's tolerance for the behaviors of individual relationships. Such sanctions are designed to establish and maintain ordinary or prosocial behaviors, depending on the desire of the principal. All relationships are different and the triggers will trip at different points, if at all, depending on the behaviors desired. For instance, while deep partnerships may be desired and rewarded in some relationships, other actors may not strive for close social interaction due to their costs and investments to build, thus there would be no trigger for rewarding prosocial behaviors, despite their occurrence. This may be the case in typical market exchange situations, where there is little need to seek longer-term relationships.

Antisocial Behaviors: This refers to intentional actions taken that harm the relationship, such as opportunism or retaliation (see Hibbard *et al.* 2001; Rokkan *et al.* 2003). Such behaviors are typically seen as intentional and may trigger some type of demotion, firing, change of boundary spanners, or relationship separation.

Although the normal reward system is designed to support ongoing exchange, many occurrences may send a relationship off

---

[1]This carrot and stick approach is typically referenced in the governance literature under the terms "extra-contractual incentives" (a carrot; Kashyap *et al.* 2012) and "enforcement" (a stick; Antia *et al.* 2006).

track. Most commonly, Pache and Santos (2010, p. 455), suggest that "compliance (is) impossible to achieve, because satisfying some demands requires defying others." The competing values problem cannot be easily solved (Groot and Merchant 2000), is faced by all controllers (Quinn and Rohrbaugh 1983), and creates tension and conflict within the relationship. Also, the actors may perceive they are being treated unfairly, which aggravates the negative effects of opportunism and conflict (Samaha *et al.* 2011). Relationships fail for many reasons, including inadequate performance, defections, and ignoring the portion of the contract that is not specifically incentivized (Prendergast 1999, Wang *et al.* 2013). Agents and other controlled parties are often self-interested, and because free riding is "each rational agent's best strategy" (Hechter 1987, p. 51), they tend to shirk by focusing on tasks that pay in the immediate term, while leaving necessary but unrewarded tasks (say, market development) uncovered. Further, monetary incentives naturally invite gaming the contract (Wathne and Heide 2000) and some business partners will inflate expenses or take unearned discounts. Such behavior is seen as antisocial and increases the transaction costs of the relationship by forcing contractually specified punishments, termination, or legal action.

Prosocial Behaviors: This supports a longer-term relationship by the parties' consideration of long-term advantages over short-term gains and losses (Kashyap and Murtha 2017). While ordinary behaviors tend to be sanctioned by the contract, extraordinary behaviors are sanctioned by the adoption of additional rules and norms. Prosocial behaviors include extra-role performance, extra effort, specific investments, the development of relational norms, and other indicators of social closeness. Increased investments and trust are some of the building blocks of longer-term exchange (Gundlach and Murphy 1993, Ring and Van de Ven 1994). Such relationship-enhancing behaviors motivate extra-contractual responses including reciprocal and expanding investments (Anderson and Weitz 1992), relational-based governance (Gilliland *et al.* 2010), and other positive behaviors (Morgan and Hunt 1994).

In summary, ordinary behaviors typically add little to the costs of control and compliance while antisocial behaviors require quite expensive remedies to realign and possibly maintain the relationship. Prosocial behaviors increase the social welfare of the parties, reducing the costs of transactions and formal compliance.

Industry norms

Over time, industries develop norms of behavior. These norms generally hold, even in changing environments and industry situations. Examples of such norms may include payment terms, shipping expectations, quality standards and standards for technical performance, customer service standards, determinants of firm success, definitions of acceptable behaviors with one another and, importantly, standard ways of doing business within and between firms (Ebers and Oerlemans 2016). When acceptable standards exist, expectations are generally shared. This reduces the need for as much formal administrative controls and safeguarding of assets (assuming reputation is important to that industry). When industry norms are in place there is less haggling over contractual details and changes. This also supports flexible changes and adaptations to changing situations (Ebers and Oerlemans 2016). Thus, depending on the industry, fewer costs may be added to those typical of formal controls, and, likewise, informal controls may reduce formal costs.

Economic and social risk

Das and Teng (2001, p. 251) suggest that, trust and control "are inextricably linked with risk." Risk is the variation in the distribution of possible outcomes from a transaction (March and Shapira 1987).

Objectively, variance is negatively associated with the attractiveness of an offer, and expected value is positively associated with attractiveness. Risk can also be thought of as the probability that a partner will not operate in good faith, creating loss. If we view risk as the probability of loss, we can consider loss from two perspectives (Das and Teng 2001). First is *economic risk*, the probability of loss of value because the venture does not execute its material expectations as specified in a contract or agreement. Failing to achieve objectives can be due to external factors to the relationship such as unexpected market entrants, unexpected economic downturns, new technologies, or the failure of the partner firm. Internal factors contributing to this risk are failures to reach an agreement, lack of relationship coordination, attempts to coerce through power, and general conflict in the relationship. In a smoothly functioning marketing channel or supply chain, operations are aligned, and tasks are efficiently executed. Failure to accomplish expected tasks detracts from the value of the relationship and results in costs that must be borne by the partner. Such economic risks are calculated considering transaction losses in revenue, time, squabbling, and other inefficiencies.

However, because all economic transactions are wrapped in a social context a social perspective on risk is considered. *Social risk* considers risk as a partner not cooperating in good faith. The social side of risk acknowledges a lack of cohesion among parties in the relationship (Das and Teng 2001). It considers a potential loss of social bonds, including affective-based commitment, loyalty, and trust. Costs related to social risk include the reduced sharing of proprietary information, mutual decision-making, and a lack of solidarity. Such losses damage the partners' ability to provide optimal efficiencies. Social risk represents uncoordinated goals due to a lack of commitment to the other party and selfish intentions. If the parties cannot align long-term interests there is little cooperation in the short term, conflict may increase, and relationship bonds are threatened. Social risk also recognizes the potential for opportunistic behavior

(Wathne and Heide 2000). As opportunism manifests, cheating and hidden actions occur and the relationship is threatened. Should the relationship break over opportunistic behaviors one of the parties may be subject to damage to their reputation, making it more difficult to collaborate with others in the future.

How Risk Motivates Control: Additional motivating factors of control are now considered. Organizations employ both formal and informal control modes. Thus, a key source of inquiry is to understand the conditions under which each is used. It is suggested that, in general, formal relationships are motivated by the extent of the firms' economic risk and informal relationships are motivated by the extent of the firms' social risk (Das and Teng 2001).

The economic risk of loss creates a situation where firms fear that contractual stipulations and obligations of a relationship will be discontinued. Such discontinuation results in instrumental assessments of the relationship's ability to survive. In order to save the contractual relationship, actors will employ formal processes to hold the contract together. Informal controls are less useful because they are based on trust, which is not initially present (Das and Teng 2001). Specific tasks will be assigned to earn adequate returns to continue the relationship (Gilliland and Manning 2002). As economic risk increases, firms will call on the codifications and stipulations of the contract to fill gaps that may be exploited by one party to escape the relationship. This requires more formal, by-the-book applications of the rules and regulations defined in the contract and calculative determinations of results. Thus, as economic risk increases there is a higher likelihood of the emergence of formal control solutions. Interestingly, as controls are followed due to formal incentives and monitoring a "thin" level of trust begins to characterize the relationship (Vosselman and Van der Meer-Koistra 2009). As the actors begin to accept trust-induced vulnerabilities, informal control — based on thickening trust and increasing social risk — is triggered and eventually grows in the relationship.

In an informal control situation, employees typically work together to achieve common goals and firms develop similarities and familiarities in vision and plans. To reduce their social risk in the relationship, they develop their own rules of understanding and norms of behavior, including the sharing of trust (Shapiro 1987). They attempt to stay socially close because of the cost efficiencies available to firms moving in the same direction. Employees from different organizations are willing to work together to resolve social differences, without the direct help of guiding contracts and seemingly arbitrary rules, which would add to confusion and cause misunderstandings, possible resentments, and inefficiencies. Instead, social exchange stamps a personalization on previously impersonal tasks (Granovetter 1985). Thus, as firms become socially closer to reduce social risk by sharing processes, guidelines and ways of doing business, they rely more on the informal rules of control.

This section has discussed how many elements of a control situation add to control costs. However, we must keep in mind that what counts is not the addition of these costs *per se*, but the *net change* in costs. For instance, when a firm is highly dependent, it must protect itself from harm by heavy monitoring, which adds monitoring costs. However, there is an overall advantage when one considers that monitoring may stop the powerful firm from taking advantage of the less powerful firm. Thus, the dependent firm's net costs of control may decrease.

Combinations of Control

Combinations of formal and informal control are an everyday occurrence. Research is interested in this rich domain of interorganizational relationships and studies have been carried out in the information management (Poppo and Zenger 2002), sales force (Cravens *et al.* 2004), accounting (Bedford 2020), and new product development (Rijsdijk and van den Ende 2011) literature. In general, such studies and others support the notion of combinations.

Basically, three exchange hazards undermine control. *Performance evaluations* consider management assessments of marketing, sales, or other personnel on a regular basis. Unfortunately, these assessments become confusing because it is difficult to relate incentives and rewards directly to productivity. Employees and boundary spanners have a tendency to shirk while taking credit in their internal reporting. Not only shirking, but more active forms of opportunistic cheating occur to take advantage of non-precise monitoring and oversight. *Uncertainty* causes other barriers which require expensive adaptations to unforeseeable changes. Technologies evolve, the environment shifts, and uncertain economies raise unexpected challenges. As changes occur, the effort–performance relationship is clouded, thus an accurate attribution of effort and success is also clouded. Finally, *specific investments* in physical and human assets demand expensive safeguarding. Because such investments are not transferrable, they are at risk of loss if precautions are not taken.

How formal and informal control modes and mechanisms combine is addressed in different ways by the different theories of governance. We examine two general conceptualizations of combination models. The first model, the *substitution model*, suggests that existing formal mechanisms such as explicit contracts, monitoring procedures, incentive, and punishment plans, are substituted under certain conditions by informal standard-setting, monitoring, and sanctioning. The *complementation model*, on the other hand, describes how formal and informal mechanisms act together in a simultaneous formation to control the partner.[2]

Substitution model of control combinations

The substitution model of control combinations is based on the concept that the least costly version of control will be adapted, which

---

[2] See Poppo and Zenger (2002) for an excellent discussion of this topic.

tends to mean that inexpensive, generally informal controls will substitute for more costly formal mechanisms. Contracts are expensive to write, negotiate, maintain, and enforce (Uzzi 1997), requiring a team of well-paid legal practitioners to keep up with constant changes in environments and dyadic situations. Monitoring, even when it is accurate, is another costly procedure, as is the payment of incentives (salaries, margins, bonuses, commissions) and the execution of specific enforcement for contractual violations. Instead of these options, less costly informal mechanisms substitute for formal mechanisms. Trust, particularly, has been examined as a replacement for formal contracts. Trust replaces expensive contracts with informal norms of doing business (Adler 2001). Larson (1992) suggests that informal relationships render formal contracts impractical and ineffective when social solutions are available. In fact, Poppo and Zenger (2002) report that Macaulay (1963, p. 64) states, "Not only are contracts and contract law not needed ... their use may have ... undesirable consequences." Macauley goes on to say that contracts may actually get in the way of social negotiations. Not only does trust avoid expensive contracting costs (Gulati 1995), trust reduces the frequency of opportunistic behaviors.

Generally, substitution can be conceptualized as a continuum of formal to informal control. As relationships become more informal, informal norms of doing business and other informal mechanisms substitute for contracts. Corporate culture and everyday relational norms substitute for contracts, monitoring is less about output and process and more about shared goals, and legal enforcement is minimized as there is less of a need for it. It should also be noted that Bernheim and Whinston (1998) modeled how formal control might substitute for informal control as well. Keeping with this thought, trust can be quite expensive to cultivate, and formal agreements may not always be so costly to implement.

This either/or approach has found empirical support in the work of Oliver and Anderson (1994) as they tested a behavioral vs. outcome salesforce control systems model. Their view of the elements of control is much broader than ours and they relate it to particular affective-based results on the behavioral side. Behavioral control is seen by the salesperson as more subjective and paternalistic while outcome controls are an objective carrot and stick program.

Thus, generally based on an economic cost argument — that is, the low-cost solution is the implemented solution — informal and formal control mechanisms may substitute for one another. The complementation model is now discussed.

Complementation Model of Control Combinations

Another perspective on combinations is offered by Poppo and Zenger (2002); formal and informal mechanisms complement one another. That is, they work together, at the same time. The belief is, "In settings where hazards are severe, the combination of formal and informal safeguards may deliver greater exchange performance than either governance choice in isolation. The presence of clearly articulated contractual terms, remedies, and processes of dispute resolution as well as relational norms of flexibility, solidarity, bilateralism, and continuance may inspire confidence to cooperate in interorganizational exchanges" (p. 712). Contracts should be clearly articulated because well-defined specification of short-run gains solidifies advantages of working together while going a long way to negate the possibilities of opportunistic behaviors. This sets the expectations that the parties to the contract will behave cooperatively in the short term, during a particularly vulnerable part of the contract. Over the longer term, informal norms and mechanisms provide for an expectation of bilateral adjustments that will protect both parties. Thus, it is the expectations of short-term and long-term success that bond the parties into a mutually operating partnership. Poppo and Zenger go on to describe that the relationship between formal and informal controls might work in reverse as well. When relationships begin to lose cohesion the formal contract stands as a way of protecting the parties as the relationship is dismantled.

Many studies, without testing for it specifically, have found support that formal and informal mechanisms operate simultaneously. Jaworski *et al.* (1993) demonstrate that control — formal and informal — can be conceptualized as a 2 × 2 matrix with formal, informal, low control (low levels of formal and informal control, and high control (high levels of formal and informal control) cells. Finally, Poppo and Zenger (2002), using a complex simultaneous estimation model, show how contractual complexity and relational norms complement one another *rather than* substitute for one another.

Combinations revisited

Given the feasibility, and reality, of control combinations, Ellickson suggests that "hybrid" control combinations are common: "When one controller would be the most promising source of rules, but another would be the cheapest enforcer of rules, controller-selecting rules might designate a hybrid form of … control" (1991, p. 242). Thus, control situations that involve multiple systems, formal and informal modes, and various control mechanisms from each mode are possible. Firms use formal contracts backed by 3rd party legal resources to hold relationships together, but they also formally monitor and, at the same time, informally build relationship norms. In fact, the notion of a single, monolithic form of control — such as formal control, or trust — is hard to comprehend. Ellickson continues, saying that the different modes and mechanisms of governance combine "in countless ways to produce hybrid systems" (1987, p. 76). Thus, as arguably broad and messy as our general hypothesis, it follows a research stream that recognizes the messiness of control, and the messiness of business exchange, and, in fact, the messiness of life.

Cost minimization also explains how hybrid systems change over time to become more complex. Consider an ongoing relationship driven by trust. As specific investments are made into the relationship, new hazards expose the parties to opportunistic behaviors. Thus, to minimize the costs of safeguarding against opportunistic behaviors (via, for instance, increased monitoring and sanctioning), a hybrid solution would be to draft new or modified formal contracts that clearly state obligations and remedies to violations. Thus, the hybrid is created. Also, this newly created hybrid will continue to morph as the situation demands, but at any given time, *the control solution in place will be the lowest-cost solution to adequately control the exchange.*

Discussion: A Quick Revisit to Formal and Informal Controls

Throughout this book, formal control has been described in various ways, including bureaucratic, hierarchical, costly, and likely to cause negative repercussions. Meanwhile, informal control has been described as efficient, productive; informal controls contain the ability to break down barriers erected by formal control, and they are necessary for long-term exchange. In fact, we calculate the *costs* of formal control and the cost *savings* of informal control. So, why do formal controls exist in the first place? Well, they wouldn't exist unless they were necessary in some way, as was pointed out at the front of the chapter.

Thus, the consideration of formal control, which has motivated most of the business scholarly research on control, is a requirement for virtually any exchange. That is, exchange would not occur without formal control. In that way, formal control is more necessary, even more important than informal control. Informal control smooths the relationship, making it more efficient and sleeker. Thus, we might say that informal control is necessary to gain competitive advantage in a market. Without formal control, costs are not minimized; costs which must be added to the price of the product that is charged downstream.

When I teach this topic, I try to advance metaphors that might better explain the relationship between formal and informal control. Consider the Dutch boy and the dike. A huge dike of formal control is built to keep out the sea and save the coast. But it is immobile, hard to modify, and can only compete with the sea in standard conditions. But when the wind blows and the power of the sea intensifies, holes would appear in the dike, and the sea of dependence structures, risk, and antisocial behaviors threaten the relationship, which the Dutch boy would plug with his hands and feet until help would arrive. Obviously, the large, monolithic, and strong dike is the formal structure on which the future of Holland rests. But there are holes in contracts, and it is through these holes that cause the failure of relationships. Perhaps informal control mechanisms such as long-term incentives and goal monitoring provide optimal conditions for filling the holes and saving the relationship.

Chapter 9

Does Control Work?

This chapter examines when and why control works and presents our second hypothesis of social control. This hypothesis examines how control is allowed to work by the target, and why the target would allow itself to be controlled.

Many of the readers want to know one thing: does control work? Well, there are three ways to answer that question: yes, no, and it depends. Unfortunately, all of these are correct. Yes, control works, otherwise, why would we go through the expense and trouble? No, control doesn't work, which might explain many failed relationships. It depends too, on one very important, and, perhaps other, intervening variables between the control mechanisms and outcomes. Clearly, it is complex, also depending on the theory, measurement, methodology, constructs, and nomology chosen to test. Also, it only makes sense that our findings are equivocal based on the many different ways that control is conceptualized (different modes, different systems, different mechanisms, different combinations).

Control, when appropriately applied, often results in positive outcomes. Control clarifies requirements, encourages conversation, provides understandable goals, keeps production on track, encourages investment, and lets the parties know when things go off course. Control can provide most of the information needed to format, guide, and execute relationships among organizations. It can also enhance communication and cooperation, and motivate the sharing of information (Frazier *et al.* 2009, Harder 1992). This has been found to result in outcomes such as better coordination, higher performance, loyalty, compliance, and decreased role ambiguity (Celly and Frazier 1996, Geyskens *et al.* 1999, Grewal *et al.* 2010, Jaworski *et al.* 1993, Kashyap *et al.* 2012, Kumar *et al.* 1995). These are all positive signs that control can improve the relationship while maintaining high standards, bottom-line success, and positively affective outcomes.

On the other hand, control can fail a relationship. Control attempts can cause confusion and be viewed as coercive. Control can be applied incorrectly, such as using a coercive and formal mechanism in a highly relational setting, or trying to monitor outcomes when adequate output information is unavailable. In these conditions and others, it is likely that the target of control could respond in a retaliatory or otherwise negative way. Not only can control increase conflict and hostility (Geyskens *et al.* 1999, Kaufmann and Stern 1988) but troublingly, control has also been found to increase opportunistic behaviors on the part of the target (Cavazos 2007, Gilliland and Kim 2014). Thus, control can have an *opposite* effect than intended. This makes the use of control in many situations akin to rolling the dice. However, we must ask if failure is due to the wrong mechanism being applied, or to an incorrect application of the correct mechanism. While incorrect applications certainly happen, I believe control failure is more often due to something else: target agreement.

Unfortunately, studies of agreement are few and far between, but Gilliland (2023) finds that outcomes are contingent on the target's agreement with control regulations. The notion of target agreement is quite important and quite logical. An organization will tend to fight back in some manner if it does not agree with how it is being controlled. Such fighting back can take many forms, as we have discussed, but these include poor attitudes and self-interest (O'Reilly 1989, Victor and Cullen 1988), which invite retaliation of some form, such as shirking and opportunistic behavior (Heide *et al.* 2007), deviant behavior, refusal to cooperate (Cavazos 2007), and even relationship exit.

Target Agreement

Target agreement is the extent that the target of control willingly accepts the controller's attempts to manage the target's outcomes and behaviors. Further, the target must agree with the controller's grounds for attempting control. This agreement can take the form of accepting the contract, monitoring scheme, incentive plan, punishment, or reasons for influence attempts. Thus, when the target agrees with the control attempts, it concedes to its control mechanisms.

Does this imply that agreement leads to success? Not really. Agreement acts as a moderator that makes it more likely to motivate an effect of control on positive outcomes, and less likely to motivate the effect of control on negative outcomes.

Where has agreement been? That is, why is it seldom covered in the extant literature? Actually, it has been used in a regulatory setting. Gilliland and Manning (2002) used agreement with regulations in a moderating condition to demonstrate the different effects of control (formal and informal) on outcomes (compliance and opportunism). While their findings were equivocal, agreement provides a path for acceptance of control attempts. Also, in a similar vein, they found that the target's acceptance of the regulator's role — that is, their positive support and appreciation of the controller, enhanced informal control attempts and constrained formal control attempts. That is, agreement and acceptance by the target affected the way that the targets were controlled. Thus, it seems clear that the target of control, in a sense, contributes to the success of the control attempts.

In the literature, agreement is generally assumed. In many cases it is assumed that if a firm monitors, the target readily acquiesces and allows itself to be monitored. If a firm provides an incentive program it is often assumed that the target agrees with the program merely because it accepts the payments. But in reality, cashing the check is quite different than judging whether the incentive is acceptable. It is likely that the target harbors resentment if it perceives unfair treatment.

But where does agreement come from? Why does a target agree with control attempt A, but not B? Let's examine this further.

When Does the Target Agree?

Our general argument is that agents will agree with the controller's attempts to control based on its costs. Agency theory is quite clear that workers will not work unless they are paid to do so. By "paid to do so," they will not work unless the net benefits of working outweigh the benefits of shirking (Bergen *et al.* 1992, Eisenhardt 1988, Hechter 1987). Thus, our second hypothesis:

If the target's benefits of acquiescing to the controller are greater than the target's benefits of shirking, the target will agree with the control attempt.

The monetary benefits[1] of acquiescing include income from the newly implemented control system. For instance, agreeing with changes to a contract may occur by examining the benefits to the new relationship structure. Perhaps the new contract allows for cost savings due to shipping, efficiencies, increased productivity, or new technology savings. Perhaps payment amounts and terms are more favorable, or resellers are provided with new products to sell. Changes in monitoring mechanisms may also be more accurate, ensuring the target is paid more or evaluated at a higher level. Increased incentives would

---

[1] Why frame the advantage as increased benefits rather than reduced costs, as was the case with the controller's decision? Because it is my belief that the controller thinks in terms of costs of implementation, such as the cost of incentives, the costs of monitoring programs, etc., while the target thinks of the benefits it may gain from control. While confusing, this cost vs. benefit approach seems to fit real-world scenarios.

be welcome in most circumstances and punishments may be thought of as offering a more equitable situation to all. For instance, in many industrial channel settings, dealers are punished for territory violations. A violator might even think that its punishment is fair because violation policies may protect it in the future. Usually, changes in informal mechanisms would be seen as potential additions to current efficiencies (less haggling over contracts and monitoring schemes).

Thus, such benefits would be compared to the benefits of shirking. Which are greater? The monetary benefits of shirking include savings from less work and effort and the ability to spend free time on other means of revenue generation, even the selling of the competitor's brand. Of course, the value of a damaged reputation must also be weighed when considering shirking. What we mean by acquiescing is to in effect, continue the relationship as defined by the control mechanism in good faith.

We have spent the bulk of the book discussing the individual pieces of control (the modes, the systems, the mechanisms). Let's now describe what an overall cycle of control might look like.

A Cycle of Control

A *cycle of control* refers to the process of recognizing the need for control, determining the control structure, the implementation of control mechanisms, the response by the target, and follow-up steps. A cycle is not constrained by time, mode of control, system of control, or implementation. In agreement with Mallen (1973), interorganizational relationships are in a constant state of change, so control cycles may be ongoing and, at least at the micro level, never-ending.

The need for control

Some form of control is needed in virtually all organizations and interorganizational relationships. Even in positive relationships, which may be driven via informal mechanisms (trust, relational exchange), changes in external environmental conditions, competitive situations, and personnel, suggest that norms must be upheld and rededicated as relationship dynamics update and present new challenges. If the costs of control do not get out of hand, there is no need to vastly change control structures.

But what happens when costs do get out of hand? There is no accountant totaling up the costs of control, but when a situation changes the general cost relationship, an organization will act to bring costs back into alignment. As an example, let's say a dealer shirks its relationship with its supplier and, instead of supporting the supplier it chooses to support the supplier's competitor. The supplier suffers lost sales as a result and the relationship with the dealer is in peril. If the cheating does not subside, the relationship will require additional control actions. Thus, whether a relationship changes its control structure is dependent on costs.

Determining the control structure

How the controller changes its control structure is also dependent on costs. As described, it will choose the low-cost solution among alternatives. Perhaps, in this example, the supplier can implement a new monitoring scheme. This scheme may catch when the reseller is shirking or being otherwise opportunistic. Of course, there are other options as well, including informal norms. Consider trust as an option. Unfortunately, trust is likely to be unavailable now that the shirking has been discovered. Trust would have to be re-earned, which may take time. It appears that, in the meantime, if trust is still the main control mechanism, the supplier is likely to be cheated again and again. Even though the new formal monitoring plan could work, it is still costly to implement. However, it may be less costly than being cheated on.

This example is certainly oversimplified. It mainly deals with the monitoring mechanism, but couldn't other mechanisms (say, punishment of some form … perhaps the dealer will lose its low-interest rate on display samples for its showroom) be applied? Of course, but which mechanism, monitoring or negative sanctions is less costly for the controller? The situation can be further complicated by the mode of control to be used. In this case it seems that formal control would apply. The final consideration would be the control system, although that would most likely not apply in this example.

Implementation of control

We have said very little here about implementing control mechanisms as this is more of a managerial topic. That said, whether control is implemented correctly or incorrectly is of vital importance. For the sake of argument, let's assume that the supplier implements a behavioral monitoring program where it puts on training sessions for the reseller and accompanies them on sales calls to ensure that the reseller is executing according to the supplier's wishes. Examining the reseller's techniques in dealing with their customers leads to more hands-on advice and possibly additional training. If the program is implemented correctly, it is likely that it will bring benefits to the reseller in terms of increased sales and possibly higher margins.

Target's assessment of benefits

Given implementation, what is the reseller's response? How does the target assess the extent that it will agree with the supplier and participate in the training and monitoring programs? The target will respond based on the benefits that it stands to gain from allowing the controller to implement the program, and how those benefits compare to the *status quo* shirking that it is currently engaged in. Thus, if the target is to agree with the monitoring scheme, the scheme must provide benefits (as claimed by the controller) such as increased sales, share, and product trial, which all result in increased margins, a distinct and real benefit. Acceptance may also spur non-monetary advantages such as a stronger working relationship, which increases efficiencies (again, increasing margins) and allows the target to anticipate the relationship as a haven over time. However, there are other benefits from shirking. The target that shirks will still receive the benefits of sales, but it will also receive benefits from spending the time learning another vendor's brand. This other vendor may have a more lucrative incentive system, a better product, an easier-to-sell product, better product support, less intrusive monitoring, a better contract, more willingness to trust, etc. Of course, the target must consider reduction in benefits from shirking including lost sales from the controller and, more significantly, the damaged reputation that accompanies being caught cheating.

In all, the target will assess the options of both positions and choose the most beneficial. That is, it will either resist the target's control attempts or go along with them. Again, by resist it may mean leaving the relationship, or it may mean maintaining the relationship with certain levels of resistance or retaliation of some form.

Now, the control profile has changed in some way between the controller and the target. New mechanisms or combinations of mechanisms may be in place, control may have changed from formal to informal or *vice versa*, in more extreme situations new controllers (say, the legal system) may have entered the picture, or new forms of retaliation or acceptance of control may now exist.

What happens next depends on the stability of the environment and the relationship. Held together by tight contracts, many franchise relationships can be stable over time, but at the same time this stability may endure much shirking and retaliation from franchisees and much coercive dealing from franchisors. Thus, just because the control characteristics are stable, it does not mean that they are optimal. But it does mean that there is some form of pressure for them to change. Certainly, franchise control would change should franchisees change the power structure in some way.

The Effect of Target Agreement

We might consider that agreement moderates the relationship between control attempts and control outcomes. When the target's agreement with the rationale for control is high (that is, it sees more benefits for control rather than against control) it allows control to occur with less chance of pushback or retribution. In this case, the relationship between the control mechanism and a positive outcome is more likely to occur than if there was low agreement. Likewise, when the target's agreement with the rationale for control is high a negative outcome is less likely to occur than if there was low agreement. On the other hand, a negative assessment of agreement suggests a greater likelihood of negative outcomes.

We have discussed the many positive and negative outcomes of control. One might wonder how the results could have changed if agreement had been considered in the models. Thus, it is important to attain the target's agreement. When agreement is lacking, it will be most unlikely for the parties to establish common ground on which to do business in a low-conflict manner. This suggests the importance of educating and training the target on the controller's position and why it must control. The more likely the target understands the arguments, the more likely it is to agree with the controller.

Profiles of Control

The notion of agreement leads our discussion to a *profile of control*. A profile of control refers to how control is manifest in the organization's daily life. This, of course, is a difficult task given the many types of control systems, modes, and mechanisms. However, simplifying control into its main components might give us a hint into how it functions.

Let us consider two key elements of control, its mode and the target's extent of agreement with the control source. As discussed previously, the elements in our consideration for agreement and control are:

- Both formal control and informal control that motivate the coordination and compliance of tasks by the target of control.
- Formal control, no matter the extent of relationalism between the controller and target, motivates some form of pushback by the target because there is resentment of being controlled. The pushback may be somewhat minor (low-level shirking) or grave (retaliation, cheating).
- There is little to no pushback to informal control by itself (there is, however, the possibility of opportunistic behavior on the part of the target if trust is high).
- High levels of target agreement with the controller (that is, its benefits from control outweigh the benefits from not being controlled) suggest that the controller is trusted, and the target is more willing to comply, while low levels of target agreement suggest that the target will resist control attempts in some form.

Table 9.1 indicates the expected interactions between control and agreement. This 2 × 2 matrix gives us an elementary expectation of the possible outcomes of the control profile. I will use the example of an environmental regulator attempting control of a for-profit firm. The regulator (controller) is interested in regulating waste disposal and environmental sustainability on a manufacturing firm (target).

Aligned control

In the bottom left cell is the condition we might refer to as *aligned control*. Aligned control is the ideal control situation for both the controller and the target of control. Relational norms via informal control drive the control aspects of the relationship and the target of control is in agreement with the control source and its objectives.

Table 9.1. Control Profiles

	Target Agreement High	Target Agreement Low
Formal Control (Standards, Monitoring, Sanctioning)	*Confounded Control* Moderate levels of: • Alignment, compliance, value creation • Retaliation and opportunism	*Coercive Control* Low levels of: • Alignment, compliance, value creation High levels of: • Retaliation and opportunism
Informal Control (Standards, Monitoring, Sanctioning)	*Aligned Control* High levels of: • Alignment, compliance, value creation Low levels of: • Retaliation and opportunism	*Acquiescent Control* Moderate levels of: • Alignment, compliance, value creation Low levels of: • Retaliation and opportunism

First, the target has determined that it is more profitable for it to conform as requested by the regulator. We can assume a situation where environmental clean-up and the application of the controller's suggestions are estimated to increase the profitability of the target. Thus, because the target is set to gain income, it is likely to agree with the controller.

When control is aligned it can be expected that the target will align itself with the demands of the controller. This works for both parties as it lowers the regulator's cost and increases the target's benefits. The target firm will comply as expected and, importantly, additional value is created. This additional value might cover many areas, but we can imagine that there is positive publicity from the change, which adds value to the target. Likewise, the health of the community might improve, and lawsuits might diminish. Again, adding value.

Further, because the relationship is driven by common goals, similar cultures, long-term orientations, and psychological contracts, retaliation is low, as is opportunism. This means less shirking, cheating, and higher levels of coordination.

Another cell that is quite rare is the coercive control cell in the upper right corner.

Coercive control

In the case of *coercive control*, there is little agreement on control and the regulator is using formal control mechanisms, which are likely considered coercive. Contracts are rigid, monitoring is intrusive, and enforcement of the contracts is by the book and unwavering. Given the rigidity of the control profile, control is seen as coercive.

Importantly, little agreement on control means that, if the firm accepted the regulator's control attempts it would be likely to enjoy fewer benefits than if it resisted control. Thus, it is likely to resist; in this case by refusing to implement the pollution abatement requirements. There is more value that can accrue to the target by fighting compliance and cooperation and not spending the money required to fix the plant. Further, they may retaliate against the regulator with lawsuits and claims of unfair treatment. They would possibly not take the steps necessary to fix the situation — in order for them to save resources — and claim that the situation was rectified. Reporting numbers might be fudged. This opportunistic and shirking behavior would supposedly provide higher levels of income for the target. However, with little cooperation, coordination, and compliance, it is likely that value creating to all the constituents in the control equation would be negative.

We can predict interesting results in the other two cells. Let's start by looking at the bottom right cell.

Acquiescent control

Acquiescent control refers to a situation where bonds drive the relationship, but rigid formal mechanisms are used by the controller. Not only is the control based on formal grounds but they are also actively executed. This seems somewhat backward in a relationship driven by informal mechanisms. If trust, long-term incentives, and soft contracts are present, why would the controller rely on formal rules?

Because the target does not agree with the source of the regulation. The target sees itself in a losing situation. However, the long-term intent of the parties may keep them together and reduce the antici-pated levels of retaliation and cheating. Still, it will occur (say, shirk-ing), as the target tries to recoup anticipated lost income. It is also expected that the target will acquiesce, in general, to the control attempts and engage in a moderate level of compliance. Thus, align-ment will also be moderate.

Confounded control

The final cell is the top left cell. This is what is known as con-founded control. *Confounded control* occurs when the target agrees with the control attempts by the regulator/controller but confounds the target's willingness to comply with formal control rules. These formal rules send the signal that the target is not trusted and must be watched and punished if it even slightly violates the contract or agree-ment. This type of control might be seen by the target as coercive and lacking goodwill and trust.

The target recognizes this confound and is likely to push back and possibly retaliate in some way. Perhaps it will hide information or fudge reports as an act of defiance. On the other hand, we know that there will be at least a moderate level of compliance and coor-dination between the two parties. Thus, the level of coordination and opportunistic behavior produce a confound to the controller's attempt to control, despite the target's agreement to the controller's requests.

The predictions of our matrix reflect the difficulty of control in this setting. Four issues should be confirmed. First, the key issue in determining the control profile is the target's extent of agreement with the source of control. This agreement is reached by assessing the benefits of the target's allowing itself to be controlled compared to the benefits if not. If the target agrees, it will want to conform to the control attempts and it may result in a more coordinated relationship. If there is no agreement and the target is forced to comply, it will retaliate in some form, despite the control mechanisms in place. Second, formal control may gain compliance from the target, but there is a cost. As we mentioned above, even when there is a high agreement between the parties, formal control may be seen as coercive and invite retaliation, shirking, and opportunism. Formal control, when used by itself, is generally not the answer. Third, true alignment is only attainable via informal control. Here, we are really discussing the aligned control cell, where informal control mechanisms are used and the target agrees with the source of control. Thus, we are discussing a rather rare opportunity when one considers the difficulty of being able to operate at a high level of informal relations. This cell is what all aspire to. The relationship is efficient, value is created, control is offered at minimum cost to the controller, and the target receives maximum benefit by agreeing to the control measures. Finally, the target must understand the benefits of control in order to fully agree. Communication must be clear so the agent makes a correct supposition about potential benefits.

Discussion: Thoughts on a Process Model for Control

We started the chapter, and the book, with a tough question: "Does control work?" We decided that it can, and in Chapter 9 we demonstrated how, even though it might be a rare set of circumstances that predict the possibility of success. Let's look back over the last few chapters and review by briefly considering a process model of control. What is the sequence of events that make up a cycle of control? That is, what happens and when, when we consider the process in which control is offered and applied, as well as the outcomes of control.

Behaviors Determine the Need for Control: The basic need for some form of control is determined by the specific behaviors of the target. Perhaps the target exhibits positive or negative behaviors that are in the realm of the ordinary. This would suggest that such actions can be handled under the standard control structure as described and enforced in the contract, enhanced by the monitoring and sanctioning system. It is when behaviors become of the extra-role variety that changes in the system are motivated. Perhaps a new contract is needed, perhaps a new monitoring system should be installed, maybe new, longer-term incentives should be introduced.

Costs of Control Determine the Control Structure: Using a minimum cost approach, the controller must wrestle with who controls; that is which control system is implemented, self-control, dyadic control, or third-party control. What mode of control is most effective, formal or informal, and finally, which individual mechanisms should be applied? However, each element in the control framework is subject to outside costs by considering the influence of the disposition of the relationship (dependence structures, etc.) industry norms, and risk. Thus, a control framework emerges.

Control Emerges: I believe the proper description of how control arises is best described as "emerges," not "is implemented." The control framework has very rigid standards but is modified naturally over time. New controllers enter or leave, modes are solidified or evolve in some way, and rules change. Is the emerging framework of intentional design or is it happenstance? Probably a bit of both as the need for control changes.

The Target Agrees or Disagrees: The target's benefits from control are assessed. Is it more beneficial to comply with control or not? Based on benefits received the target may wish to be controlled — perhaps it allows a haven from environmental changes and competitive pressures — or perhaps it can earn more benefits by shirking.

A Control Profile is Installed: A certain, hopefully stable, combination of control mechanisms is applied to the control situation. System, mode, and mechanisms emerge or are installed in some way. Based on the installation of the new control profile, personal and professional relationships may also be modified or changed. New people and organizations may enter the picture due to the changing situation. Trust may have to be re-established from scratch as new relationships form.

The Target Reacts to Control: Based on its level of agreement with the control efforts — which is based on the net benefits of control — the target responds in a variety of ways. It may conform to control and anticipate positive benefits from its actions. Or it may push back in some way: retaliation, opportunistic behavior, or shirking. It is through this process that control might be considered successful or unsuccessful.

Control Reassessment: Control is most likely reassessed on a continual basis, suggesting control may change continually. Feedback loops from the target's response to behavior and control may lead to changes including new controllers, modes, and mechanisms.

The process identified seems logical and clear. However, if it were so, we would see many more control success stories. Instead, control may be irrational based on actions by the actors and nonlinear in implementation. All are part of the complexities of control.

Chapter 10

What Next?

I hope our discussion of the origins, derivations, applications, and success of control has been interesting, and I further hope that drawing your attention to the development of social control theory has been worthwhile. Social control is studied in most all business applications as well as other social sciences such as sociology, anthropology, and psychology. The perspectives of each have added a specific view on the overall aspects of what it means to control and be controlled. In our case, we have found control to be the anchor of business relationships, both organizational, interorganizational, and third party.

Control is, admittedly, much too broad to squeeze into 180 pages and a few diagrams. However, this modest attempt at gathering our knowledge of control, creating a framework, and considering the use of this framework, may push us forward. Hopefully, this multisystem perspective will allow us to think of the hegemonic nature of control. As I said in the first sentence of this book, "control is ubiquitous." Not only is control ubiquitous in a business organization sense but it can also help explain personal and family relationships, broad social and political movements, crime and punishment, and more.

Where to from here? The new framework may outline a path, or paths, to new knowledge. Hopefully, this text has shed some light on how the need for control is started in business relationships, how control is formulated based on the costs of the specific mechanisms in use, how it is applied, how it is evaluated by the targets of control, and, just possibly, whether control works or not. We may also know a bit more about how control changes with time, and why. With this knowledge in hand, might we go further?

As a body of researchers, we must establish the domain of control in business organizations. Where, precisely, does the front end of governance give way to a control-dominated back end? Who controls who; just how many steps down the channel of distribution does an OEM supplier's ability to control stretch? How powerful is the role of power? These and many other questions need answers. Further, we must carefully organize, classify, define, and measure the various aspects of control. Finally, we must rigorously test the links in the models presented here. There is obviously a slew of antecedent, consequent, moderating, and mediating conditions to uncover. For instance, what conditions enhance coordination and mitigate conflict? Does conflict run from simple passive shirking to retaliation, and what do the differences depend on? Then, there are the questions surrounding combinations (substitution, complementation, both) and their effects. Are combinations successful, or are they just attempts at a high level of control without knowledge or consideration of outcomes? Finally, how do formal and informal control fit into our lexicon of relational norms, market exchange, unilateral and bilateral governance, trust, and the like? Much interesting work is to be done.

First, it was made clear by Krafft's (1999) examination of various governance types that not all theories predicted similar outcomes nor did they have similar antecedent and consequent conditions. How might re-examination of the governance literature through the lens of control be beneficial? Once clear predictors and outcomes of control are established, perhaps the existing literature should be reviewed to determine if a control perspective could help explain unexpected or non-significant findings. That is, how robust is our theory of control?

The various patterns of control should be documented and veri-fied. Control can be vertical downstream and upstream as in an OEM/dealer relationship. It can be part of a large network of organi-zations, as in a Japanese *keiretsu*. It can be horizontal as in a regula-tory relationship. Further, it can be based on the dependence of one party on the other. Can the less-powered party control the more powerful? What about control in highly risky conditions; how does control change based on pattern? Does control vary upstream and down, does control vary despite the level of power? In other words, can you turn the control framework "upside-down" and recognize the same results? These are various patterns of control that each beg a plethora of questions about how control works and doesn't work.

Control, from our perspective, is more than dyadic, it considers first- and third-party conditions. Regarding first-party control, a true social control perspective suggests that control starts with self-help. Self-help is generally seen as a mechanism to protect oneself. Thus, if a psychological contract between a firm and an employee is broken, it seems logical that the employee might take their talents elsewhere. This moving elsewhere, or reacting in some less abrupt way, means that self-help is manifest as specific behavior, which starts the cycle of control as described in the process model in Chapter 9. Without self-help, there would be no control. But is self-help as simple as acting? What about another employee in the same situation who doesn't take action? Importantly, what characteristics or situational conditions motivate the act of self-help, and how might that affect our model of control?

The basic control mechanisms, setting standards, monitoring, and sanctioning are how the work gets done in the organization. Each mechanism plays its part in the overall control picture in its attempt to increase efficiencies and productivities. But do, and if so how, do these mechanisms change across various modes and systems? That is, are the mechanisms stagnant or dynamic? Is output monitoring just that, despite how the overall structure (say, dominated by informal norms instead of formal contracts) may change? Further, what happens during combinations of control? Does the same formal monitoring mechanism exist in its same rigid way? Is the same information interpreted differently and results in the same response to the target of control? Does outcome monitoring change with antecedent levels (say, a great deal of trust) or does it stay the same? Or, maybe just the interpretation of the data changes.

In fact, recent work has focused on the dynamic nature of marketing relationships (Jap and Anderson 2007, Palmatier *et al.* 2013, Zhang *et al.* 2016). In general, their premise is that marketing relationships change in a variety of ways; they are not stagnant. They change with time, with personnel changes, and with increasing or decreasing levels of relational norms and trust. Two questions arise. First, how do the mechanisms change as a relationship is modified across time? As the parties become closer or more distant, how does the same monitoring program mentioned above adjust? We can also look at this question with another lens; how do the mechanisms of control change the structure of the relationship? As various control mechanisms are implemented, what becomes of those personal relationships that the relationship is founded upon?

Although combinations of control have been discussed in Chapter 8, there is much more to learn about this interesting phenomenon. Basically, control can combine by both system and mode. In either case, the clashing of the various aspects of the relationship will likely have some effect on the control mechanisms currently operating in the relationship. For instance, as the formal and informal modes of control combine (see Jaworski *et al.* 1993), the mechanisms will change in nature. Consider that the formal monitoring mechanisms could be replaced by informal. This, of course, seldom happens instantly, thus formal mechanisms with its focus on output and behavior may clash with the norm- and goal-based monitoring of informal control mechanisms. Control may further change by system as controllers are added to the mix. Say a dyad is troubled by legal interpretations of a contract. What happens when the court system stands in the middle of the relationship? Does control cease, pause, or change in some other way?

In Chapter 8, I suggest that everyday behaviors are a large part of control. The literature has mainly investigated control as specific actions that take place, which can potentially change the control structure in some way. But a large part of the time control is stable as designed. It does not mean that control is non-existent or does not work, it means that control often holds as is, guided by the standards established in the relationship. While it seems simple, there is still much to investigate. For instance, just how far out of line must ordinary behavior be to attain the level of non-ordinary? What fills the holes in the standards (via the contract or other agreements) at the everyday level, norms? If so, are these relational norms, or is there an entirely different set of norms that we might label as *everyday norms*? Does everyday behavior contribute in a positive way to enhance relationships, and if so, how? What happens when everyday relationships go awry?

One of the more interesting aspects of contemporary control studies considers the dark side of control (see Anderson and Jap 2005). There are two elements here that raise our curiosity regarding control. First, as we have discussed, even in relationships described as trusting, many non-relational elements sometimes remain such as opportunistic behaviors, cheating, taking advantage of information asymmetries, and more. This is attributed to the trusted party letting its guard down and allowing its partner to operate without adequate monitoring. Second, there may be many more unintended consequences of creating a dark side in a seemingly solid partnership. Such consequences (probably coercive formal control mechanisms) can poison a relationship even when the parties are operating by the book. Consider competitive encroachment, disruptive challenges to the existing contract, upsetting environmental conditions, and other circumstances that may threaten the *status quo*.

The Technology of Control: The Final Frontier or a New Beginning?

As we enter the age of artificial intelligence, business organizations are analyzing how they might make the most of new technologies.[1] AI, blockchain, drones and GPS, digital trackers, machine learning, biometrics, and more promise the possibilities of increased productivity and across-the-board efficiencies. What does this mean for organizational control? Will our theories be affected by the new age of microelectronic tools?

It seems that most of the governance-related changes that should be discussed might come under the moniker of *micro-monitoring*. Micro-monitoring involves the monitoring of employee output and behaviors by electronic means. Let's briefly discuss how micro-monitoring might affect control.

First, we must acknowledge the vast speed at which micro-monitoring advancements are being made. Thus, what we discuss today might be obsolete soon.

In most cases, micro-monitoring refers to monitoring aspects of employees, not so much organizations. Micro-monitoring provides the firm with additional levels of information on which decisions can be made regarding sanctions (both positive and negative) that might be provided to the employees.

A few examples of micro-monitoring include:

- On-board computers monitor vehicle operators' trip, operator, and vehicle details to ensure safety and productivity of the driver.
- Biometric sensors that identify personnel based on fingerprint, facial, iris, voice recognition, and hand geometry.
- 3D cameras for object and gesture recognition.

---

[1] The author thanks Richard Zhen Tang, Avishek Lahiri, Paige Fender, Jody Crosno, and Steve Kim for their excellent insights and contributions in this section.

- Drones use aerial photography for inventory control and geographic mapping.
- GPS technology via satellite tracking systems.
- Social media and website monitoring tools such as keystroke logs and website tracking to ensure employee productivity.
- Wearables such as smart watches and glasses, which track physiological fitness and location.

These technologies are already being used in the trucking, heavy construction machinery, and call-center industries. Micro-monitoring allows electronic confirmation of employee activities and accomplishments. The use of such technologies might be classified as formal monitoring, which allows information gathering of both outcome and behavioral activities. However, although the information is reliable and documented, there may be other considerations for the use of this formal control mechanism. Let's consider information from both the controller and target's position.

For the controller, it has a constant stream of information that allows it to more accurately determine performance. This can be used to reward/punish the employee as well as to learn about human behavior and how jobs are actually accomplished. One might imagine the information allows the setting of benchmarks and can be used for training and best practices guidelines. For the target, however, there may be few positive outcomes (except achievement-based information). Instead, the employee might feel unfairly watched and be fearful that the accrued information would be used to punish certain behaviors or even that the controller would be interested in replacing them with yet more technology such as driverless trucks and AI customer support.

Thus, what is important is the effect of the information. Clearly, it is positive for the controller, at least in the short term. But what about over time, when employees may revolt by refusing to be monitored, changing their behaviors in some way, or by somehow gaming the system? We may refer to this dilemma as the "hidden cost of micro-monitoring." Formal control always has a substantive cost of compliance, and this may be an example of such costs.

In summary, will micro-monitoring change control theoretically, or is it just another mechanism used to gather monitoring information? Most likely the latter, although one might imagine a temporal dimension to control, where the speed of monitoring and the ability to monitor new areas may affect costs and interpretations of data.

Our journey ends. In conclusion, the multisystem control perspective provides a compelling framework for organizing the broad domain of control. It also allows consideration of social control as a meta-theory for understanding complex governance relationships. Social control has been at the core of this book, allowing us a basic understanding of new control events and organizing the extant literature, explaining additional events, and suggesting avenues of future research pursuit.

References

Acemoglu, D., Kremer, M. & Mian, A. (2008). Incentives in Markets, Firms and Government. *The Journal of Law, Economics, and Organization*, 24 (2), 273–306.

Achrol, Ravi S. (1996). Changes in the Theory of Interorganizational Relations in Marketing: Toward a Network Paradigm, *Journal of the Academy of Marketing Science*, 25 (1), 56–71.

Adams, J. S. & Freedman, S. (1976). Equity Theory Revisited: Comments and Annotated Bibliography. *Advances in Experimental Social Psychology*, 9, 43–90.

Adler, P. S. (2001). Market, Hierarchy and Trust: The Knowledge Economy and the Future of Capitalism. *Organization Science*, 12 (2), 215–234.

Akerlof, G. A. & Kranton, R. E. (2005). Identity and the Economics of Organizations. *Journal of Economic Perspectives*, 19 (1), 9–32.

Allen, N. J. & Meyer, J. P. (1996). Affective, Continuance, and Normative Commitment to the Organization: An Examination of Construct Validity. *Journal of Vocational Behavior*, 49 (3), 252–276.

Anderson, E. & Jap, S. (2005). The Dark Side of Close Relationships. *Sloan Management Review*, 46 (3), 75–82.

Anderson, E., Lodish, L. M. & Weitz, B. A. (1987). Resource Allocation Behavior in Conventional Channels. *Journal of Marketing Research*, 24, 85–97.

Anderson, E. & Oliver, R. L. (1987). Behavior and Outcome-Based Sales Control Systems: Evidence and Consequences of Pure Form and Hybrid Governance. *Journal of Marketing*, 51 (4), 76–88.

Anderson, E. & Weitz, B. A. (1992). The Use of Pledges to Build and Sustain Commitment in Distribution Channels. *Journal of Marketing Research*, 29 (1), 18–34.

Antia, K. D., Bergen, M. E., Dutta, S. & Fisher, R. J. (2006). How Does Enforcement Deter Grey Market Incidence? *Journal of Marketing*, 70 (January), 92–106.

Antia, K. D. & Frazier, G. L. (2001). The Severity of Contract Enforcement in Interfirm Channel Relationships. *Journal of Marketing*, 65 (October), 67–81.

Antia, K. D., Zheng, X. & Frazier, G. L. (2013). Conflict Management and Outcomes in Franchise Relationships: The Role of Regulation. *Journal of Marketing Research*, 50 (October), 577–589.

Bachmann, R. (2001). Trust, Power and Control in Trans-Organizational Relations. *Organization Studies*, 22 (2), 337–365.

Baker, G. (2002). Distortion and Risk in Incentive Contracts. *The Journal of Human Resources*, 37, 728–751.

Barney, J. B. & Hansen, M. H. (1994). Trustworthiness as a Source of Competitive Advantage. *Strategic Management Journal*, 15, 175–216.

Bedford, D. S. (2020). Conceptual and Empirical Issues in Understanding Management Control Combinations. *Accounting, Organizations and Society*, 86, 1–8.

Bello, D. C. (2011). International Distribution Channels. In J. Sheth & N. Malhotra (Eds.), *Wiley International Encyclopedia of Marketing*, 6, 107–114. West Sussex, UK: John Wiley & Sons.

Bello, D. C. & Gilliland, D. I. (1997). The Effect of Output Controls, Process Controls and Flexibility on Export Channel Performance. *Journal of Marketing*, 61 (January), 22–38.

Benabou, R. & Tirole, J. (2003). Intrinsic and Extrinsic Motivation. *The Review of Economic Studies*, 70, 489–520.

Bergen, M., Dutta, S. & Walker, O. C. Jr. (1992). Agency Relationships in Marketing: A Review of the Implications and Applications of Agency and Related Theories. *Journal of Marketing*, 56, 1–24.

Bernheim, B. D. & Whinston, M. D. (1998). Incomplete Contracts and Strategic Ambiguity. *American Economic Review*, 88 (4), 902–932.

Bijlsma-Frankema, K. M. & Costa, A. C. (2005). Understanding the Trust-Control Nexus. *International Sociology*, 20 (3), 259–282.

Black, D. (1976). *The Behavior of Law*. New York: Academic Press.

Black, D. (1998). *The Social Structure of Right and Wrong*. San Diego: Academic Press.

Blattberg, R. C. & Neslin, S. A. (1990). *Sales Promotion: Concepts, Methods and Strategies*. Englewood Cliffs, NJ: Prentice Hall.

Bouillon, M. L., Ferrier, G. D., Stuebs Jr., M. T. & West, T. D. (2006). The Economic Benefit of Goal Congruence and Implications for

Management Control Systems. *Journal of Accounting and Public Policy*, 25, 265–298.

Braddach, J. L. & Eccles, R. G. (1989). Price Authority and Trust: From Ideal Types to Plural Forms. *Annual Review of Sociology*, 15, 97–118.

Braithwaite, J. (2002). Rewards and Regulation. *Journal of Law and Society*, 29 (1), 12–26.

Braithwaite, J., Walker, J. & Grabosky, P. (1987). An Enforcement Taxonomy of Regulatory Agencies. *Law and Policy*, 9 (3), 323–351.

Braithwaite, V. (2007). Responsive Regulation and Taxation: Introduction. *Law and Policy*, 29 (1), 3–10.

Brown, J. R., Cobb, A. T. & Lusch, R. F. (2006). The Roles Played by Interorganizational Contracts and Justice in Channel Relationships. *Journal of Business Research*, 59, 166–175.

Buchanan, L. (1992). Vertical Trade Relationships: The Role of Dependence and Symmetry in Attaining Organizational Goals. *Journal of Marketing Research*, 29 (February), 65–75.

Caldwell, D. F. & O'Reilly III, C. A. (1990). Measuring Person-Job Fit with a Profile-Comparison Process. *Journal of Applied Psychology*, 75 (6), 648–657.

Cannon, J. P. & Homburg, C. (2000). Buyer–Supplier Relationships and Customer Firm Costs. *Journal of Marketing*, 65 (January), 29–43.

Cao, Z. & Lumineau, F. (2015). Revisiting the Interplay between Contractual and Relational Governance: A Qualitative and Analytic Investigation. *Journal of Operations Management*, 33–34, 15–32.

Carson, S. J. & Ghosh, M. (2019). An Integrated Power and Efficiency Model of Contractual Channel Governance: Theory and Empirical Evidence. *Journal of Marketing*, 83 (4), 101–120.

Carter, R. C. (2000). Ethical Issues in International Buyer–Supplier Relationships: A Dyadic Examination. *Journal of Operations Management*, 18 (2), 191–208.

Cavazos, D. E. (2007). Capturing the Regulatory Rule Making Process: How Historical Antecedents of U.S. Regulatory Agencies Impact Industry Conditions. *International Journal of Organizational Analysis*, 15 (3), 231–250.

Celly, K. S. & Frazier, G. L. (1996). Outcome-Based and Behavior-Based Coordination Efforts in Channel Relationships. *Journal of Marketing Research*, 33, 200–210.

Chen, D., Park, S. H., & Newbury, W. (2009). Parent Contribution and Organizational Control in International Joint Ventures. *Strategic Management Journal*, 30, 1133–1156.

Coase, R. (1937). The Nature of the Firm. *Economica*, 4 (16), 386–405.

Conroy, S. A. & Gupta, N. (2016). Team Pay-for-Performance: The Devil is in the Details. *Group and Organization Management*, 4 (1), 32–65.

Cravens, D. W., Lassk, F. G., Low, G. S., Marshall, G. W. & Moncrief, W. C. (2004). Formal and Informal Management Control Combinations in Sales Organizations: The Impact on Salesperson Consequences. *Journal of Business Research*, 57, 241–248.

Crosno, J. L. & Brown, J. R. (2015). A Meta-Analytic Review of the Effects of Organizational Control in Marketing Exchange Relationships. *Journal of the Academy of Marketing Science*, 43, 297–314.

Dahlstrom, R. & Nygaard, A. (1999). An Empirical Investigation of *Ex-Post* Transaction Costs in Franchised Distribution Channels. *Journal of Marketing Research*, 32 (2), 160–170.

Das, T. K. & Teng, B. S. (2001). Trust, Control, and Risk in Strategic Alliances: An Integrated Framework. *Organization Studies*, 22, 2, 251–283.

Deci, E. L., Koestner, R. & Ryan, R. M. (1999). A Meta-Analytic Review of Experiments Examining the Effects of Extrinsic Rewards on Intrinsic Motivation. *Psychological Bulletin*, 125, 627–668.

Deci, E. L. & Ryan, R. M. (1980). The Empirical Exploration of Intrinsic Motivation Processes. In L. Berkowitz (Ed.), *Advances in Experimental Social Psychology*, 13, 39–80. New York: Academic.

Deci, E. L. & Ryan, R. M. (2000). The "What" and "Why" of Goal Pursuits: Human Needs and the Self-Determination of Behavior. *Psychological Inquiry*, 11 (4), 227–268.

Dekker, H. C. (2004). Control of Inter-Organizational Relationships. *Accounting, Organizations and Society*, 29 (1), 27–49.

Doney, P. M. & Cannon, J. P. (1997). An Examination of the Nature of Trust in Buyer–Seller Relationships. *Journal of Marketing*, 61 (2), 35–51.

Dwyer, F. R., Schurr, P. H. & Oh, S. (1987). Developing Buyer–Seller Relationships. *Journal of Marketing*, 51 (2), 11–27.

Dyer, J. H. & Singh, H. (1998). The Relational View: Cooperative Strategy and Interorganizational Competitive Advantage. *Academy of Management Review*, 23 (4), 660–679.

Ebers, M. & Oerlemans, L. (2016). The Variety of Governance Structures Beyond Market and Hierarchy. *Journal of Management*, 42 (6), 1491–1529.

Eisenhardt, K. M. (1988). Control: Organization and Economic Approaches. *Management Science*, 31 (February), 134–149.

Eisenhardt, K. M. (1989). Agency Theory: An Assessment and Review. *Academy of Management Review*, 14 (January), 57–74.

Eisenhardt, K. (1985). Control: Organizational and Economic Approaches. *Management Science*, 31 (2) 134–149.

Ellickson, R. C. (1987). A Critique of Economic and Sociological Theories of Social Control. *Journal of Legal Studies*, 16, 67–99.

Ellickson, R. C. (1991). *Order Without Law: How Neighbors Settle Disputes*. Massachusetts: Harvard University Press.

Emsley, D. & Kidon, F. (2007). The Relationship Between Trust and Control in International Joint Ventures: Evidence from the Airline Industry. *Contemporary Accounting Research*, 24 (3), 829–858.

Fang, E., Palmatier, R. W., Scheer, L. K. & Li, N. (2008). Trust at Different Organizational Levels. *Journal of Marketing*, 72 (March), 80–98.

Farnsworth, E. A. (1982). *Contracts*. Boston: Little Brown.

Fayol, H. (1949). *General and Industrial Management*, translated by C. Storrs. Marshfield, MA: Pitman. Originally published in French in 1916.

Fehr, E. & Gachter, S. (2000). Fairness and Retaliation: The Economics of Reciprocity. *Journal of Economic Perspectives*, 14 (3), 159–181.

Feltham, G. A. & Xie, J. (1994). Performance Measure Congruity and Diversity in Multi-Task Principal/Agent Relationships. *The Accounting Review*, 69, 429–453.

Fites, D. V. (1996). Make Your Dealers Your Partners. *Harvard Business Review*, 74 (2), 84–95.

Frazier, G. L. (1983). On the Measurement of Interfirm Power in Channels of Distribution. *Journal of Marketing Research*, 20 (2), 158–166.

Frazier, G. L. (1984). The Interfirm Power-Influence Process Within a Marketing Channel. *Research in Marketing*, 7, 63–91.

Frazier, G. L., Gill, J. D. & Kale, S. H. (1989). Dealer Dependence Levels and Reciprocal Actions in a Channel of Distribution in a Developing Country. *Journal of Marketing*, 53 (1), 50–69.

Frazier, G. L., Maltz, E., Antia, K. D. & Rindfleisch, A. (2009). Distributor Sharing of Strategic Information with Suppliers. *Journal of Marketing*, 73(4), 31–43.

Frazier, G. L. & Summers, J. (1984). Interfirm Influence Strategies and Their Application Within Distribution Channels. *Journal of Marketing*, 48 (Summer), 38–48.

French, J. R. & Raven, B. H. (1959). The Bases of Social Power. In D. Cartwright (Ed.), *Studies in Social Power*, 150–167. Ann Arbor: Institute for Social Research.

Frey, B. S. (1993). Does Monitoring Increase Work Effort? The Rivalry with Trust and Loyalty. *Economic Inquiry*, 31 (October), 663–670.

Ganesan, S. (1994). Determinants of Long-Term Orientation in Buyer–Seller Relationships. *Journal of Marketing*, 58 (2), 1–19.

Garcia, A. (2015). Amazon's Culture is "Purposeful Darwinism". https://money.cnn.com/2015/08/15/technology/amazon-new-york-times/.

Gargiulo, M. & Ertug, G. (1996). The Dark Side of Trust. In Bachman and Zaheer (Eds.), *Handbook of Trust Research*, 165–168. Cheltenham: Edward Elgar.

Geyskens, I., Steenkamp, J.-B. E. M. & Kumar, N. (1999). A Meta-Analysis of Satisfaction in Marketing Channel Relationships. *Journal of Marketing Research*, 36, 221–238.

Gibbons, R. (2005). Incentive Between Firms (and Within). *Management Science*, 51, 2–17.

Gibbs, J. P. (1989). *Control: Sociology's Central Notion*. Illinois: University of Illinois Press.

Gilliland, D. I. (2003). Toward a Business-to-Business Channel Incentives Classification Scheme. *Industrial Marketing Management*, 32, 55–67.

Gilliland, D. I. (2023). A Multi-System Organizing Framework for Inter-Firm Control: A Comprehensive Perspective on Control. *Journal of the Academy of Marketing Science*, 51, 6–85.

Gilliland, D. I. & Bello, D. C. (2002). Two Sides to Attitudinal Commitment: The Effect of Calculative and Loyalty Commitment on Enforcement Mechanisms in Distribution Channels. *Journal of the Academy of Marketing Science*, 30 (1), 24–43.

Gilliland, D. I., Bello, D. C. & Gundlach, G. T. (2010). Control-Based Channel Governance and Relative Dependence. *Journal of the Academy of Marketing Science*, 38, 441–455.

Gilliland, D. I. & Kim, S. K. (2014). When Do Incentives Work in Channels of Distribution? *Journal of the Academy of Marketing Science*, 42, 361–379.

Gilliland, D. I. & Manning, K. C. (2002). When Do Firms Conform to Regulatory Control? The Effect of Control Processes on Compliance and Opportunism. *Journal of Public Policy & Marketing*, 21, 319–331.

Grabosky, P. N. (1995). Regulation by Reward: On the Use of Incentives as Regulatory Instruments. *Law and Policy* 17 (3), 257–282.

Granovetter, M. (1985). Economic Action and Social Structure: The Problem of Embeddedness. *American Journal of Sociology*, 91 (3), 481–510.

Greenberger, D. B. & Strasser, S. (1986). Development and Application of a Model of Personal Control in Organizations. *The Academy of Management Review*, 11 (1), 164–177.

Grewal, R., Chakravarty, A. & Saini, A. (2010). Governance Mechanisms in Business-to-Business Electronic Markets. *Journal of Marketing*, 74, 45–62.

Grewal, R., Kumar, A., Mallapragada, G. & Saini, A. (2013). Marketing Channels in Foreign Markets: Control Mechanisms and the Moderating Role of Multinational Corporation Headquarters-Subsidiary Relationship. *Journal of Marketing Research*, 50 (June), 378–398.

Griffith, D. A. & Zhou, Y. (2015). Contract Specificity, Contract Violation, and Relationship Performance in International Buyer–Supplier Relationships. *Journal of International Marketing*, 23 (3), 22–40.

Groot, T. L. C. M. & Merchant, K. A. (2000). Control of International Joint Ventures. *Accounting, Organizations and Society*, 25, 579–607.

Grove Human Resources.com (2022). Inside Netflix Company Culture: Amazing and Unusual. https://blog.grovehr.com/netflix-company-culture#:~:text=Freedom%20and%20Responsibility,to%20make%20 the%20best%20decision.

Gulati, R. (1995). Does Familiarity Breed Trust: The Implications for Repeated Ties for Contractual Choices in Alliances. *Academy of Management Journal*, 38 (1), 85–112.

Gulati, R. & Nickerson, J. A. (2022). Interorganizational Trust, Governance Choice, and Exchange Performance. *Organization Science*, 19 (5), 688–708.

Gundlach, G. T. & Cadotte, E. R. (1994). Exchange Interdependence and Interfirm-Interaction: Research in a Simulated Channel Setting. *Journal of Marketing Research*, 31 (November), 516–532.

Gundlach, G. T. & Cannon, J. P. (2010). "Trust by Verify"? The Performance Implications of Verification Strategies in Trusting Relationships. *Journal of the Academy of Marketing Science*, 38, 399–417.

Gundlach, G. T. & Murphy, P. E. (1993). Ethical and Legal Foundations of Relational Marketing Exchanges. *Journal of Marketing*, 57, 35–46.

Hakobyan, A. & E. Team (2022). Company Culture at Google. www.emex-mag.com/company-culture-at-google/.

Harder, J. W. (1992). Play for Pay: Effects of Inequity in a Pay for Performance Context. *Administrative Science Quarterly*, 37 (2), 321–335.

Hawkins, K. (1984). *Environment and Enforcement: Regulation and the Social Definition of Pollution*. New York: Oxford University Press.

Hechter, M. (1987). Principles of Group Solidarity. In Michael Hechter (Ed.), *Principles of Group Solidarity*. Berkeley: University of California Press.

Heide, J. B. (1994). Interorganizational Governance in Marketing Channels. *Journal of Marketing*, 58, 71–85.

Heide, J. B., Bell, S. J. & Tracy, P. (2022). Who We Are and How We Govern: The Effect of Identity Orientation on Governance Choice. *Journal of Marketing*, 87 (1), 45–63.

Heide, J. B. & John, G. (1990). Alliances in Industrial Purchasing: The Determinants of Joint Action in Buyer–Supplier Relationships. *Journal of Marketing Research*, 27 (1), 24–36.

Heide, J. B. & John, G. (1992). Do Norms Matter in Marketing Relationships? *Journal of Marketing*, 56, 32–44.

Heide, J. B., Kumar, A. & Wathne, K. H. (2011). Performance Implications of Mismatched Governance Regimes Across External and Internal Relationships. *Journal of Marketing*, 75 (March), 1–17.

Heide, J. B. & Wathne, K. H. (2006). Friends, Businesspeople, and Relationship Roles: A Conceptual Framework and a Research Agenda. *Journal of Marketing*, 70 (July), 90–103.

Heide, J. B., Wathne, K. H. & Rokkan, A. I. (2007). Interfirm Monitoring, Social Contracts, and Relationship Outcomes. *Journal of Marketing Research*, 44, 425–433.

Hibbard. J. D., Kumar, N. & Stern, L. W. (2001). Examining the Impact of Destructive Acts in Marketing Channel Relationships. *Journal of Marketing Research*, 38 (February), 45–61.

Hollinger, R. C. & Clark, J. P. (1982). Formal and Informal Social Controls of Employee Deviance. *The Sociological Quarterly*, 23 (3), 333–343.

Holmstrom, B. & Milgrom, P. (1991). Multitask Principal–Agent Analyses: Incentive Contracts, Asset Ownership, and Job Design. *The Journal of Law, Economics, and Organization*, 7 (Special Issue), 24–52.

Holmstrom, B. & Milgrom, P. (1994). The Firm as an Incentive System. *American Economic Review*, 84, 972–991.

Hsu, A. & Selyukh A. (2022). Union Wins Made Big News This Year. *NPR*, https://www.npr.org/2022/12/27/1145090566/labor-unions-organizing-elections-worker-rights-wages.

Hunt, S. D. (1991). *Modern Marketing Theory: Critical Issues in the Philosophy of Marketing Science*. Cincinnati: South-Western Publishing Co.

Jackson, B. B. (1985). Build Customer Relationships that Last. *Harvard Business Review*, 11, 120–128.

Janowitz, M. (1975). Sociological Theory and Social Control. *American Journal of Sociology*, 81 (1), 82–108.

Jap, S. & Anderson, E. (2007). Testing a Life-Cycle Theory of Cooperative Interorganizational Relationships: Movement Across Stages and Performance. *Management Science*, 53 (2), 260–275.

Jaworski, B. J. (1988). Toward a Theory of Marketing Control: Environmental Context, Control Types, and Consequences. *Journal of Marketing*, 52, 23–39.

Jaworski, B. J., Stathakopoulas V. & Krishnan, H. S. (1993). Control Combinations in Marketing: Conceptual Framework and Empirical Evidence. *Journal of Marketing*, 57, 57–59.

Jenkins, G. D. Jr., Mitra, A., Gupta, N. & Shaw, J. D. (1998). Are Financial Incentives Related to Performance? A Meta-Analytic Review of Empirical Research. *Journal of Applied Psychology*, 83 (5), 777–787.

Jensen, M. & Meckling, W. (1976). Theory of the Firm: Managerial Behavior, Agency Costs and Capital Structure. *Journal of Financial Economics*, 3 (October), 305–360.

Job, J., Stout, A. & Smith, R. (2007). Culture Change in Three Taxation Administrations: From Command and Control to Responsive Regulation. *Law and Policy*, 29 (1), 84–101.

Johnston, W. J. & Bonoma, T. V. (1981). The Buying Center: Structure and Interaction Patterns. *Journal of Marketing*, 45 (3), 143–156.

Kashyap, V., Antia, K. D. & Frazier, G. L. (2012). Contracts, Extra-Contractual Incentives, and Ex Post Behavior in Franchise Channel Relationships. *Journal of Marketing Research*, 49, 260–276.

Kashyap, V. & Murtha, B. R. (2017). The Joint Effects of *Ex Ante* Contractual Completeness and *Ex Post* Governance on Compliance in Franchised Marketing Channels. *Journal of Marketing*, 81 (3), 130–153.

Kaufmann, P. J. & Stern, L. W. (1988). Relational Exchange Norms, Perceptions of Unfairness, and Retained Hostility in Commercial Litigation. *The Journal of Conflict Resolution*, 32, 534–552.

Kerr, S. (1975). On the Folly of Rewarding A, While Hoping for B. *Academy of Management Journal*, 18, 769–783.

Khan, I. U., Khan, M. S. & Khan, H. (2020). The Role of Procedural Justice in Connecting the Contingent Punishments and Employees' Responsiveness. *Sir Syed Journal of Education and Social Research*, 3 (1), 217–226.

Kim, S. K., McFarland, R. G., Kwon, S., Son, S. & Griffith, D. A. (2011). Understanding Governance Decisions in a Partially Integrated Channel, a Contingent Alignment Framework. *Journal of Marketing Research*, 48 (3), 603–616.

Klein, H. J. (1989). An Integrated Control Theory Model of Work Motivation. *Academy of Management Review*, 14 (2) 150–172.

Klein, S., Frazier, G. & Roth, V. J. (1990), A Transaction Cost Analysis Model of Channel Integration in International Markets. *Journal of Marketing Research*, 27 (May), 196–208.

Kleinaltenkamp, M., Eggert, A., Kashyap, V. & Ulaga, W. (2022). Rethinking Customer-Perceived Value in Business Markets from an Organizational Perspective. *Journal of Inter-Organizational Relationships*, 28(1–2), 1–18.

Kohn, M. (1988). The Finance Constraint Theory of Money: A Progress Report. *The Jerome Levy Economics Institute Working Paper*, (5).

Krafft, M. (1999). An Empirical Investigation of the Antecedents of Sales Force Control Systems. *Journal of Marketing*, 63 (July), 120–134.

Kumar, A., Heide, J. B. & Wathne, K. H. (2011). Performance Implications of Mismatched Governance Regimes Across External and Internal Relationships. *Journal of Marketing*, 75, 1–17.

Kumar, N., Scheer, L. K. & Steenkamp, J.-B. E. M. (1995). The Effects of Supplier Fairness on Vulnerable Resellers. *Journal of Marketing Research*, 33 (February), 43–65.

Lado, A. A., Dant, R. R. & Tekleab, A. G. (2008). Trust-Opportunism Paradox, Relationalism, and Performance in Interfirm Relationships: Evidence from the Retail Industry. *Strategic Management Journal*, 29, 401–423.

Lai, A. W. & Nevin, J. R. (1995). *Interorganizational Behavior Controls: A Theoretic Framework*. Working Paper. Madison: University of Wisconsin.

Lange, D. (2008). A Multidimensional Conceptualization of Organizational Corruption Control. *Academy of Management Review*, 33 (3), 710–729.

Larson, A. (1992). Network Dyads in Entrepreneurial Settings: A Study of the Governance of Exchange Relationships. *Administrative Science Quarterly*, 37, 76–104.

Lazear, E. P. (2000). The Power of Incentives. *American Economic Review*, 90, 410–414.

Lazear, E. P. & Oyer, P. (2013). Personnel Economics. In R. Gibson and J. D. Roberts (Eds.), *Handbook of Organization Economics*, 479–519. Princeton: Princeton University Press.

Lazzarini, S. G., Miller, G. J. & Zenger, T. R. (2004). Order with Some Law: Complementarity vs. Substitution of Formal and Informal Arrangements. *Journal of Law, Economics, and Organization*, 20 (October), 261–298.

Liao, C., Wayne, S. J. & Rousseau, D. M. (2016). Idiosyncratic Deals in Contemporary Organizations: A Qualitative and Meta-Analytical Review. *Journal of Organizational Behavior*, 37, S9–S29.

Lindgreen, A., Hingley, M. K., Grant, D. B. & Morgan, R. (2012). Value in Business and Industrial Marketing: Past, Present, and Future. *Industrial Marketing Management*, 41 (1), 207–214.

Lo, D., Ghosh, M. & Lafontaine, F. (2011). The Incentive and Selection Roles of Sales Force Compensation Contracts. *Journal of Marketing Research*, 48 (4), 781–798.

Locke, E. A. & Latham, G. P. (1990). Work Motivation and Satisfaction: Light at the End of the Tunnel. *Psychological Science*, 1 (4), 240–246.

Lumineau, F. (2017). How Contracts Influence Trust and Distrust. *Journal of Management*, 43 (5), 1553–1577.

Luneneberg, F. C. (2012). Power and Leadership: An Influence Process. *International Journal of Management, Business and Administration*, 15 (1), 1–9.

Lusch, R. F. & Brown, J. R. (1996). Interdependency, Contracting, and Relational Behavior in Marketing Channels. *Journal of Marketing*, 60, 19–38.

Macaulay, S. (1963). Non-Contractual Relations in Business: A Preliminary Study. *American Sociological Review*, 28 (1), 55–67.

Macneil, I. R. (1980). *The New Social Contract: An Inquiry into Modern Contractual Relations*. New Haven, CT: Yale University Press.

Mallen, B. (1973). Functional spin-off: A key to anticipating change in distribution structure. *Journal of Marketing*, 37 (3), 18–25.

Manz, C. C. (1986). Self-Leadership: Toward an Expanded Theory of Self-Influence Processes in Organizations. *The Academy of Management Review*, 11, 585–600.

March, J. G. & Shapira, Z. (1987). Managerial Perspectives on Risk and Risk Taking. *Management Science*, 33 (11), 1404–1418.

May, P. J. (2005). Regulation and Compliance Motivations: Examining Different Approaches. *Public Administration Review*, 65 (1), 31–44.

McFarland, R. G., Bloodgood, J. M. & Payan, J. M. (2008). Supply Chain Contagion. *Journal of Marketing*, 72 (2), 63–79.

Merchant, K. W. (1988). Progressing Toward a Theory of Marketing Control: A Comment. *Journal of Marketing*, 53 (January), 70–79.

Mishra, D. P., Heide, J. B. & Cort, S. G. (1998). Information Asymmetry and Levels of Agency Relationships. *Journal of Marketing Research*, 35 (3), 277–295.

Mooi, E. A. & Ghosh, M. (2010). Contract Specificity and Its Performance Implications. *Journal of Marketing*, 74 (2), 105–120.

Mooi, E. A. & Gilliland, D. I. (2013). How Contracts and Enforcement Explain Transaction Outcomes. *International Journal of Research in Marketing*, 30, 395–405.

Mooi, E. & Stefan, W. (2021). Value from Technology Licensing — The Role of Monitoring and Licensing Experience. *International Journal of Research in Marketing*, 38 (4), 1034–1054.

Morgan, R. M. & Hunt, S. D. (1994). The Commitment–Trust Theory of Relationship Marketing. *Journal of Marketing*, 58 (July), 20–38.

Mukherji, A., Wright, P. & Mukherji, J. (2007). Cohesiveness and Goals in Agency Networks: Explaining Conflict and Cooperation. *The Journal of Socio-Economics*, 36, 949–964.

Murry, J. P. & Heide, J. B. (1998). Managing Promotion Program Participation Within Manufacturer–Retailer Relationships. *Journal of Marketing*, 62 (1), 58–68.

Nielsen, V. L. & Parker, C. (2012). Mixed Motives: Economic, Social and Normative Motivations in Business Compliance. *Law and Policy*, 34 (4), 428–462.

O'Reilly, C. (1989). Corporations, Culture, and Commitment: Motivation and Social Control in Organizations. *California Management Review*, Summer, 9.

O'Reilly, C. A. & Chatman, J. A. (1996). Culture as Social Control: Corporations, Cults, and Commitment. In B. M. Staw & L. L. Cummings

(Eds.), *Research in Organizational Behavior: An Annual Series of Analytical Essays and Critical Reviews*, 18, 157–200. Elsevier Science/JAI Press.

Obadia, C., Bello, D. C. & Gilliland, D. I. (2015). Effect of Exporter's Incentives on Foreign Distributors' Role Performance. *Journal of International Business Studies*, 46, 960–983.

Oliver, R. L. & Anderson, E. (1994). An Empirical Test of the Consequences of Behavior-and Outcome-Based Sales Control Systems. *Journal of Marketing*, 58 (4), 53–67.

Oliviera, N. & Lumineau, F. (2019). The Dark Side of Interorganizational Relationships: An Integrative Review and Research Agenda. *Journal of Management*, 45 (1), 231–261.

Ouchi, W. G. (1979). A Conceptual Framework for the Design of Organizational Control Mechanisms. *Management Science*, 25 (9), 833–848.

Ouchi, W. G. & Maguire, A. M. (1975). Organizational Control: Two Functions. *Administrative Science Quarterly*, 20 (December), 559–569.

Oyer, P. (1998). Fiscal Year Ends and Nonlinear Incentive Contracts: The Effect on Business Seasonality. *The Quarterly Journal of Economics*, 113 (1), 149–185.

Pache, A. C. & Santos, F. (2010). When Worlds Collide: The Internal Dynamics of Organizational Responses to Conflicting Institutional Demands. *Academy of Management Review*, 35 (3), 455–476.

Palmatier, R. W., Houston, M. B., Dant, R. P. & Grewal, D. (2013). Relationship Velocity: Toward a Theory of Relationship Dynamics. *Journal of Marketing*, 77 (January), 13–30.

Payan, J. M. & McFarland, R. G. (2005). Decomposing Influence Strategies: Argument Structure and Dependence as Determinants of the Effectiveness of Influence Strategies in Gaining Channel Member Compliance. *Journal of Marketing*, 69, 66–79.

Pfeffer, J. & Salancik, G. (2003). *The External Control of Organizations: A Resource Dependence Perspective*. Stanford, CA: Stanford University Press.

Poppo, L. & Zenger, T. (2002). Do Formal Contracts and Relational Governance Function as Substitutes or Complements? *Strategic Management Journal*, 23 (8), 707–725.

Prendergast, C. (1999). The Provision of Incentives in Firms. *Journal of Economic Literature*, 37, 7–63.

Quinn, R. E. & Rohrbaugh, J. A. (1983). A Spatial Model of Effectiveness Criteria: Towards a Competing Values Approach to Organizational Effectiveness. *Management Science*, 29, 363–377.

Rajwani, T., Lawton, T. & Phillips, N. (2015). The "Voice of Industry": Why Management Researchers Should Pay More Attention to Trade Associations. *Strategic Organization*, 13 (3), 224–232.

Rhoades, L. & Eisenberger, R. (2002). Perceived Organizational Support: A Review of the Literature. *Journal of Applied Psychology*, 87 (4), 698–714.

Rijsdijk, S. A. & van den Ende, J. (2011). Control Combinations in New Product Development Projects. *Journal of Product Innovation Management*, 28, 868–880.

Rindfleisch, A. & Heide, J. B. (1997). Transaction Cost Analysis: Past, Present, and Future Applications. *Journal of Marketing*, 61, 30–54.

Ring, P. S. & Van de Ven, A. H. (1994). Developmental Processes of Cooperative Interorganizational Relationships. *Academy of Management Review*, 19, 90–118.

Robinson, S. L. & Rousseau, D. M. (1994). Violating the Psychological Contract: Not the Exception but the Norm. *Journal of Organizational Behavior*, 15 (3), 245–259.

Rokkan, A. I., Heide, J. B. & Wathne, K. H. (2003). Specific Investments in Marketing Relationships: Expropriation and Bonding Effects. *Journal of Marketing Research*, 40 (2), 210–224.

Rousseau, D. M. (1989). Psychological and Implied Contracts in Organizations. *Employee Responsibilities and Rights Journal*, 2 (2), 121–139.

Rubin, P. H. (1990). *Managing Business Transactions: Controlling the Cost of Coordinating, Communicating, and Decision Making*. New York, NY: The Free Press.

Ryan, R. M. & Deci, E. L. (2000). Self-Determination Theory and the Facilitation of Intrinsic Motivation, Social Development, and Well-Being. *American Psychologist*, 55, 68–78.

Samaha, S. A., Beck, J. T. & Palmatier, R. W. (2014). The Role of Culture in International Relationship Marketing. *Journal of Marketing*, 78, 78–98.

Samaha, S. A., Palmatier, R. W. & Dant, R. P. (2011). Poisoning Relationships: Perceived Unfairness in Channels of Distribution. *Journal of Marketing*, 75 (May), 99–117.

Scheer, L. K., Kumar, N. & Steenkamp, J.-B. E. (2003). Reactions of Perceived Inequity in US and Dutch Interorganizational Relationships. *Academy of Management Journal*, 46 (3), 303–316.

Scheer, L. K., Miao, C. F. & Palmatier, R. W. (2015). Dependence and Interdependence in Marketing Relationships: Meta-Analytic Insights. *Journal of the Academy of Marketing Science*, 43, 694–712.

Schleicher, D. J., Baumann, H. M., Sullivan, D. W., Levy, P. E., Hargrove, D. C. & Barros-Rivera, B. A. (2018). Putting the *System* into Performance Management Systems: A Review and Agenda for Performance Management Research. *Journal of Management*, 44 (6), 2209–2245.

188   *The Control of Business Relationships*

Schoorman, F. D., Mayer, R. C. & Davis, J. H. (2007). An Integrative Model of Trust: Past, Present and Future. *Academy of Management Review*, 32 (2), 344–354.

Scott, A. & Connelly, L. B. (2011). Financial Incentives and the Health Workforce. *Australian Health Review*, 35 (3), 273–277.

Selnes, F. & Sallis, J. (2003). Promoting Relationship Learning. *Journal of Marketing*, 67 (3), 80–95.

Shapiro, S. P. (1987). The Social Control of Impersonal Trust. *American Journal of Sociology*, 93 (3), 623–658.

Shipilov, A. V., Li, S. X. & Greve, H. R. (2011). The Prince and the Pauper: Search and Brokerage in the Initiation of Status-Heterophilous Ties. *Organization Science*, 22 (6), 1418–1434.

Sinclair, D. (1997). Self-Regulation Versus Command and Control? Beyond False Dichotomies. *Law and Policy*, 19 (4), 529–559.

Slater, P. (1980). *Wealth Addiction*. New York: Dutton.

Tomkins, C. (2001). Interdependencies, Trust and Information in Relationships, Alliances and Networks. *Accounting, Organization and Society*, 26 (2), 161–191.

Tönnies, F. ([1887] 1957). *Community and Society*. New Jersey: Transaction Publishers, 43, 226–229.

Uzzi, B. (1997). Social Structure and Competition in Interfirm Networks. *Administrative Science Quarterly*, 42 (1), 37–69.

van der Kolk, B., van Veen-Dirks, P. M. G. & ter Bogt, H. J. (2020). How Combinations of Control Elements Create Tensions and How These Can Be Managed: An Embedded Case Study, *Management Accounting Research*, 48, 1–15.

van Knippenberg, D. (2000). Work Motivation and Performance: A Social Identity Perspective. *Applied Psychology: An International Review*, 49 (3), 357–371.

Victor, B. & Cullen, J. B. (1988). The Organizational Basis of Ethical Work Climate. *Administrative Science Quarterly*, 33, 101–125.

Villena, V. H., Revilla, E. & Choi, T. Y. (2011). The Dark Side Of Buyer–Supplier Relationships: A Social Capital Perspective. *Journal of Operations Management*, 29 (6), 561–576.

Vosselman, E. & van der Meer-Kooistra, J. (2009). Accounting for Control and Trust Building in Interfirm Transactional Relationships. *Accounting, Organizations and Society*, 34, 267–283.

Vroom, V. H. (1964). *Work and Motivation*. Hoboken: Wiley.

Wang, D. T., Gu, Flora, F. & Dong, M. C. (2013). Observer Effects of Punishment in a Distribution Network. *Journal of Marketing Research*, 50 (5), 627–643.

Wasserman, N. (2006). Stewards, Agents, and the Founder Discount: Executive Compensation in New Ventures. *Academy of Management Journal*, 49, 960–976.

Wathne, K. H. & Heide, J. B. (2000). Opportunism in Interfirm Relationships: Forms, Outcomes, and Solutions. *Journal of Marketing*, 64, 36–51.

Wathne, K. H. & Heide, J. B. (2004). Relationship Governance in a Supply Chain Network. *Journal of Marketing*, 68 (1), 73–89.

Weiner, R. R. (2011). The Changing Forms of Contracting in a Society of Transnational Networks. *TELOScope*.

White, H. (1985). Agency as Control. In J. Pratt and R. J. Zeckhauser (Eds.), *Principals and Agents: The Structure of Business*, 187–212. Boston: Harvard Business School Press.

Williamson, O. E. (1975). *Markets and Hierarchies: Analysis and Antitrust Implications*. New York: The Free Press.

Williamson, O. E. (1991). Comparative Economic Organization: The Analysis of Discrete Structural Alternatives. *Administrative Science Quarterly*, 36, 269–296.

Williamson, O. E. (1996). *The Mechanisms of Governance*. New York: Oxford University Press.

Winter, S. & May, P. J. (2001). Motivation for Compliance with Environmental Regulations. *Journal of Policy Analysis and Management*, 20, 675–698.

Wuyts, S. & Geyskens, I. (2005). The Formation of Buyer–Seller Relationships: Detailed Contract Drafting and Close Partner Selection. *Journal of Marketing*, 69 (October), 103–117.

Wuyts, S., Stremersch, S., Bulte, C. V. D. & Frances, P. H. (2004). Vertical Marketing Systems for Complex Products: A Triadic Perspective. *Journal of Marketing Research*, 4, 479–487.

Zaheer, A., McEvily, W. & Perrone, V. (1998). Does Trust Matter: Exploring the Effects of Interorganizational and Interpersonal Trust on Performance. *Organization Science*, 9, 141–159.

Zaheer, A. & Venkatraman, N. (1994). Determinants of Electronic Integration in the Insurance Industry: An Empirical Test. *Management Science*, 40 (5), 549–566.

Zhang, J. Z., Watson IV, G. F., Palmatier, R. W. & Dant, R. P. (2016). Dynamic Relationship Marketing. *Journal of Marketing*, 80 (September), 53–75.

Zhong, R. & Robinson, S. L. (2021). What Happens to Bad Actors in Organizations? A Review of Actor-Centric Outcomes of Negative Behavior. *Journal of Management*, 47 (6), 1430–1467.

Zucker, L. G. (1986). Production of Trust: Institutional Sources of Economic Structure 1840–1920. In L. L. Cummings and B. Staw (Eds.), *Research in Organizational Behavior*, 8, 55–111. Greenwich, Conn: JAI.

Index

Printed in the United States
by Baker & Taylor Publisher Services